When It's Hard to Forgive

When It's Hard to Forgive

Goldie Bristol
with Carol McGinnis

This book is designed for your personal reading pleasure and profit. It is also designed for group study. A leader's guide with helps and hints for teachers and visual aids (Victor Multiuse Transparency Masters) is available from your local bookstore or from the publisher.

VICTOR BOOKS

a division of SP Publications, Inc.
WHEATON. ILLINOIS 60187

Offices also in Fullerton, California • Whitby, Ontario, Canada • Amersham-on-the-Hill, Bucks, England

Unless otherwise noted, Scripture quotations are from the *New International Version,* © 1978 by the New York International Bible Society. Other quotations are from the *King James Version* (KJV). Used by permission.

Recommended Dewey Decimal Classification: 248.4
  Suggested Subject Headings: CHRISTIAN LIFE: FORGIVENESS; EMOTIONS

Library of Congress Catalog Card Number: 81-86288
ISBN: 0-88207-311-7

VICTOR BOOKS
A division of SP Publications, Inc.
P.O. Box 1825 • Wheaton, Illinois 60187

Contents

To our parents:
Mrs. Orpha Schurman, for her loving and faithful teaching
of God's Word and the practice of it in her daily life,
and
James and Elaine McGinnis, for their loving support.

Foreword

Reading the *New York Times* one day back in 1978, my eye caught the headline of an unusual story. Parents of a vivacious 21-year-old girl who had been raped and murdered 8 years earlier, had paid a personal visit to a California prison to embrace their daughter's murderer in forgiveness.

Three years before their visit, on learning that the assailant had been apprehended and sentenced to life imprisonment, they had written to him. They told him that they had no bitterness, but had forgiven him because Christ had forgiven them their sins. Several weeks passed before a cautious reply came. In the ensuing correspondence, the parents asked permission to pay him a visit, which he granted.

Reaction to such forgiveness has varied from admiring amazement to angry disapproval that such a person should be forgiven. In *When It's Hard to Forgive,* Goldie Bristol, the mother of the victim (with co-author Carol McGinnis) tells her moving story. This book deals with the theme of forgiveness from every angle, showing that Christians should forgive others completely—all the time—no matter whom the offender, and no matter what the offense. Though other people may not accept *our* forgiveness, it should be available. Emotion-packed illustrations of forgiveness add to the book's impact.

It has been my delightful privilege to meet Mrs. Bristol. She claims to speak not as an authority, but as an example. What an example, especially to those of us who find it difficult to forgive even the mildest of slights!

DR. LESLIE B. FLYNN
PASTOR, GRACE CONSERVATIVE BAPTIST CHURCH
NANUET, NEW YORK

Introduction

I am not a theologian. Or a psychiatrist. But I am a child of God and I am constantly learning to be more like Him.

God has been teaching me some valuable lessons: facts I had too long overlooked or ignored; biblical principles that should characterize each of our lives and become a vital part of our daily living; attitudes which the Holy Spirit would so much like to lift from the pages of Scripture and incorporate into our moment by moment walk with Christ.

One lesson is the importance of forgiveness. Jesus commands it. I have always known that, but before November 17, 1970 I paid little attention to it. I had not been forced in a serious way to really face the issue until my husband and I received word of our daughter's rape and murder. I cried. I hurt. I poured out my anguish to God. And He was there comforting, gently placing His forgiveness for our daughter's murderer into our wounded hearts. It was a miracle! It was rewarding...freeing...exciting!

In the years since Diane's death, God has been teaching me much about forgiveness. I have learned forgiveness is necessary for our emotional, physical, and spiritual well-being. I have learned how forgiveness heals and changes both the offended one and the offender. I certainly am not, nor ever will be, the epitome of forgiveness or *the* authority on the subject. Yet I cannot help but speak and write of the truth God is showing me to be so vitally important: Christian forgiveness.

After writing *These Tears Are for Diane* (Word) and receiving subsequent speaking engagements and correspondence, I've discovered that most people don't share my enthusiasm. Some Christians are as guilty as non-Christians of being cold, calloused, and often seemingly unconcerned.

I am also perplexed at the lack of teaching on the Christian's responsibility to forgive. There is much material on God's forgiveness for men and women and that is good. Without understanding that, we really can't know how to forgive each other. But I find very little on the subject of Christians totally forgiving others—no matter whom the offender and no matter what the offense. For these reasons, I want to spread what God is teaching me as far and wide as possible.

To readers who want to adopt a forgiving attitude, I offer two suggestions. First approach the subject with an open mind and take the time to really see what the Bible has to say. Before your thoughts and lives can be changed, there must be a willing spirit that says, "Lord, You show me. You teach me. I need Your help to give and forgive." If you make this your motto, the process of becoming more Christlike will be much less painful.

Writing a book is never a solitary process. Many others have contributed their thoughts and ideas to this work. Many have prayed. It would be impossible to thank everyone, but I would especially like to mention:

- My co-author, Carol McGinnis. She has been a faithful and dedicated asset to this work. Her interest, time, research, and writing skills have been invaluable.
- My husband, Bob, who has been an excellent critic and has been completely supportive all these months.
- My editor, Becky Dodson, and all the other great people at Victor Books who have helped make this book possible.
- All those who have allowed their personal stories to be shared.
- All those who took the time from busy schedules to send, by request, helpful information.
- And all those who prayed for the completion of this venture.

GOLDIE BRISTOL

*   *   *

When Goldie Bristol asked me to co-author a book on

12

forgiveness, I hesitated. I had once read that God will not place a pen into a writer's hand to explain His truths until the writer has first learned them. I knew I wasn't a particularly forgiving person and I wondered if I would be willing to learn forgiveness.

It took me two weeks to reach a decision. During that time I prayed, I talked with several people, and I spent time thinking—not just about what it would mean to write a book, but what it would mean to write *this* book. The Apostle Paul and the Apostle James both tell us that it is through suffering and being tested that we develop our patience (Rom. 5:3; James 1:2-3). I suspected the same principle would hold true when it came to learning forgiveness.

I was right.

Soon after agreeing to work on this book the problems, the offenses, and the hurts began—on the job, with friends, and with family. God gave me several opportunities to learn to be forgiving. Sometimes I succeeded; more often I failed. Through it all, I've learned—but by no means have I mastered forgiveness.

I've learned something else too. This book contains a message that's needed. Society is hostile and forgiveness is uncommon. Long ago the Apostle Paul described the days in which we live:

> People will be lovers of themselves, lovers of money, boastful, proud, abusive, disobedient to their parents, ungrateful, unholy, without love, unforgiving, slanderous, without self-control, brutal, not lovers of the good, treacherous, rash, conceited, lovers of pleasure rather than lovers of God (2 Tim. 3:2-4).

As we approach the end of this age, there will be more and more opportunities to be forgiving. Christians should be ready to show an unbelieving world what the forgiving love of Jesus Christ really means.

CAROL McGINNIS

It's strange how
the person I can't stand,
whose very name can start
my mind reeling in hostility,
is the very person
who controls my life.

I don't leave him
where he hurt me,
But in my heart
I drag him home with me.
I take him into my room
and spend time with him
in my thoughts,
where he dominates.
He rules my tongue,
influencing me to lash out
at those I love,
because he burns me up.
And soon, he's taken command
of my attitudes and actions,
and I am consumed.

How often the fire of hate
does more damage to the hater,
than to his target.

O Lord, please pour Your cooling love
on my heated heart,
as I leave at Your feet
all the hurts that I have harbored.

LINDA KLING

1
We Forgave Our Daughter's Killer

"For My thoughts are not your thoughts, neither are your ways My ways," declares the Lord. "As the heavens are higher than the earth, so are My ways higher than your ways and My thoughts than your thoughts" (Isa. 55:8-9).

January, 1978

The wipers running full speed struggled to keep the windshield clear in the driving rain. Rain had been pouring for hours, slowing our pace and dampening our spirits.

My husband Bob and I watched for road signs and landmarks and kept checking over the directions to avoid making wrong turns. Suddenly there it was . . . the prison . . . looking formidable as it loomed into view through the rain. The many buildings, fences, and gates seemed to cover a lot of land.

We saw what appeared to be the main entrance and turned into the drive, hoping to find a parking space near the door. But parking spaces close by had large signs, NO PARKING and RESERVED. We knew we would have to run through the rain with the wind trying to whisk us away.

That might not be such a bad idea, I thought, as I began

15

growing apprehensive. Very soon we would meet the man who seven years before had raped and murdered our daughter.

Diane

We had received the news via telegram of Diane's sudden and violent death Wednesday, November 18, 1970. It had been a busy day. That afternoon I had prepared pumpkin pie and sweet potatoes for our church's annual Harvest Dinner. As I loaded the food in the car, the phone rang.

I was tempted to ignore it, but better judgment told me to answer the phone. When I picked up the receiver, a voice from Western Union read a telegram from the San Diego County Coroner: "REGRET TO INFORM YOU OF DEATH OF DAUGHTER DIANE. PLEASE ADVISE AS TO DISPOSITION OF BODY."

I couldn't believe what I had heard. Could it be someone's idea of a joke? I asked to have the message repeated. But I had heard right. My daughter was dead.

Hot and cold waves started at my head and rushed to my feet. I had never felt such a sickening sensation. Numbly, I dialed my husband's phone number at work. Thousands of thoughts flashed through my mind. *How had she died? Was it an accident? Murder? Suicide? Where had it happened? Why? When?*

My husband answered his phone right away. He was as shocked as I, and said he'd be right home. I sat to wait for him, groping in tears, toward God in prayer. The Harvest Dinner and food in my car were forgotten.

When my husband arrived home, he called the San Diego County Coroner. We learned that Diane had been raped and murdered the night before. Her partially clothed body had been found lying in a driveway in East San Diego. Diane had been selling encyclopedias when she was attacked; she had gotten the job only 10 days before.

We later learned her assailant, a stranger to her and her friends, had planned his strategy well. He had apparently been watching and following Diane as she moved from house to house. The police told us when she reached a secluded area, he grabbed her from behind. Because of the bruises on her body, we assume that a struggle ensued. Later we learned that when her assailant heard of her death on the news the next morning, he was surprised and frightened. He had not expected her to die. All his other victims had survived.

Diane had been 21 years old, a vivacious, 5'4" blond with a full life ahead of her. She had concluded a wonderful two month visit with us just three weeks before. But now she was gone, her life snuffed out in moments.

My husband Bob and I have two sons, Rollie and David, who were older than Diane. They both came home as soon as they heard the news. We are a Christian family; we had been for some time. Our faith was deeply rooted in God through Jesus Christ, but that didn't exempt us from this heart-rending tragedy. Our reactions were very normal, very human ones . . . deep anguish, heartbreak, and tears.

Relatives, friends, and even neighbors we hardly knew came to our home to give us their support. Some brought food; some sat with us and wept. Some suggested I take sedatives or tranquilizers, but I was sure I didn't need any.

Various friends quoted over and over Romans 8:28-29 to me. These were sincere and loving friends who wanted desperately to show that they cared and could empathize with us. However, I wasn't ready for those Scriptures then. I was hurting much too much and the words just didn't take hold in my heart.

But in the midst of our emotional disarray, I did sense the presence and the love of the "God of all comfort" (2 Cor. 1:3). True to His word, He was there! He dispensed His grace, comfort, strength, love, and acceptance . . . continuously . . . as it was needed. And it was always enough! Yet my pain was *so* deep. There is no describing the "torn apart" feeling that existed in my heart. I had never hurt so deeply and painfully before.

I was glad I knew God intimately and could draw from His ample provisions made for those of us who will trust Him implicitly (Phil. 4:6, Eph. 3:20). I knew He loved me; I knew He loved Diane; I knew He understood the deep groaning in my heart, and that He was in complete control. I didn't question God. In my extreme sorrow, I took comfort (Heb. 4:16) in His everlasting arms (Deut. 33:27).

Six months before Diane's death, I prayed a special prayer. Diane had strayed from God for a couple of years. She became a Christian at age 10, was involved with the church, youth groups, and summer camps. I am sure she loved Jesus Christ with all her heart. But during her teens she began to doubt her faith; she had questions she didn't feel were adequately answered.

She left home in January, 1969 stayed in Hawaii for six months, then moved to California. She adopted a lifestyle characteristic of many of the youth of that day.

In May, 1970 at a Bible study and prayertime, I had prayed, "God please bring Diane back to Yourself, in Your way, for Your honor and glory."

Then in August, 1970 Diane wrote to Bob and me requesting we stay out of her life (for now she was 21). She said she would straighten out her life and she hoped we would straighten out ours. Bob and I were crushed, but we decided to respect her request. We knew God would continue to work in her life.

Diane came home unexpectedly Labor Day weekend, 1970, just two weeks after making that request. We welcomed her with open arms. She explained that she felt compelled to come home.

During her two-month visit, Diane shared her life with us, openly and honestly. She had been struggling to discover who she was and what she should do with her life. She told us of her relationship with her boyfriend Brad. But most important, she told us she had reached some conclusions about herself and God.

She had reevaluated the plans she had previously set aside. She could sing, for she realized that God had given her a lovely voice. She would pursue her studies in music.

During those two months at home, Diane spent much time visiting friends—everyone from high school teachers and counselors to her college roommate and old neighbors. This was something else she said she felt compelled to do. She spent hours reading the Bible and recording her thoughts in her journal.

On October 26, Diane boarded a plane bound for San Diego. She said she loved us and that she might be back by Christmas if she didn't get a job and settle down in San Diego. At any rate, I was happy and felt confident God had her in His hands.

We received a cheerful note from Diane three weeks later. She had severed her tie with Brad; she had found a job. "I believe my life is pointed in the right direction at last," she wrote. That same afternoon we received the telegram telling us of her death.

Even as I heard that telegram, I remembered my prayer from six months before. I believed my prayer had been answered . . . not in a way I would have chosen, but in God's way for His purposes. I didn't ask Him why. I knew I could trust Him. He loved me and He loved Diane. But knowing this did not ease my anguish.

Forgiveness

Finally I began to experience a degree of emotional stability again. I went to God with all the hurts of my heart and said, "Father, I don't know what to do with so heavy a burden. . . . Will You take the sorrow of my heart and use it for Your honor and glory? Please make something good, something beautiful out of it all, as only You can do. May it promote spiritual growth in my own life . . . more love for You, for Your Word and for Your people, both saved and unsaved, both lovely and unlovely."

I knew I could do nothing in and of myself, but with God all things are possible. He took me at my word, for our family embarked on a spiritual expansion program which has been, and still is, overwhelming to me.

First I noticed that as a family we were praying for our daughter's killer. He certainly needed Jesus Christ in his life. We prayed for him regularly and often.

Surprisingly we found that we weren't filled with resentment. We were not in bondage to him, but, miraculously, filled with the freedom of forgiveness instead. Incomprehensible? Impossible? Many have thought so. But "nothing is impossible with God" (Luke 1:37).

Does this sound unrealistic? Super-spiritual? It isn't really. God simply chose some very ordinary people to perform His miracle of forgiving love. We *know* He did this because our reactions to our daughter's assailant have not been the normal and expected kind. For His reasons and purposes, God chose to place in our hearts His miracle of forgiveness for a man toward whom many people . . . even believers . . . would choose to seek revenge.

Interestingly, I could not pray for my daughter's murderer regularly, whoever he might be and wherever he was, without beginning to love him and care about what was happening to him. Certainly, as a family, we did not condone his action. He had committed a serious crime before God and society and to our family in particular.

Why this interest? We knew the Bible taught, as does the law of our land, that a criminal act should be punished and paid for, and we believed this. Yet God was helping us to see this criminal as a person, made in God's own image, one created with the capacity to love and serve God. We were capable of seeing value and worth in him—an immortal soul that was worth saving.

"What good will it be for a man if he gains the whole world, yet forfeits his soul?" Jesus asked (Matt. 16:26). Our prayer for Diane's killer became a constant one, that whoever he was, he would not experience the wages of sin which is death, but rather, the gift of God which is eternal life through Jesus Christ our Lord (Rom. 6:23).

Dear Tom

Approximately three years after Diane's death, her assailant was apprehended, tried, and sentenced to life in prison. Our interest in him increased. We now knew his name and where he was located. Would it be possible to let him know what God had so miraculously done for us?

I contacted Prison Mission Association, Inc. in Riverside, California, telling the director, Joe Mason, of our desire to communicate with Tom.* Mr. Mason wrote to Tom telling him of our desire to share God's love with him and to tell him we held no bitterness toward him. Tom answered Mr. Mason right away, asking if he might correspond with us indirectly through the mission.

My first letter to Tom was dated October 22, 1975. I wrote:
> You have not just accidentally been placed in our pathway. There is a definite purpose in it, a "God-planned arrangement," I believe. . . .

I assured him that we held no bitterness toward him, *attributing it as a miracle from God.* Briefly, I shared the plan of salvation. I offered to send him a Bible and I promised we would be praying for him.

A few weeks passed and no response came. Several more weeks slipped by before I realized what a shock my letter must have been to Tom. The mother of the girl he had murdered was writing him, telling him she was not bitter. He must have wondered if my letter was truthful, if I had a hidden motive for writing. Realizing it might be difficult for him to respond, I wrote again and told him we would understand if he felt he could not write to us.

Finally, in January we received an answer. He thanked us for our kindness and our Christian example, and he told us a little of his background. From that cautious beginning, our correspondence blossomed. We learned to know one another. We became friends. It meant so much to him, even though he could not comprehend that we were praying for him . . . that we had forgiven him. He could not figure that out.

I shared my faith with Tom. In one early letter I wrote:
> In our eagerness to be of encouragement and help, we don't ever, in any way want to "turn you off" . . . I hope and pray this low point in your life does turn

---
*Not his real name.

your thinking God-ward. . . . Please may you ever
remember that God has brought our paths together
for some great reason of His own and we are in
constant prayer that *His reason* will be realized.

Gradually Tom opened his heart and shared some of his
deepest thoughts, though this was difficult for him. I assured
him that we had not initiated this correspondence in order to
learn more about Diane's death. In May, 1976 I wrote:

I wish we could visit face to face, there is less
possibility for misunderstanding. Anyway, if you
have sensed that . . . our motives in writing you are to
gain 'information' regarding Diane, please set your
mind at rest. . . . We have believed that very possibly
we know all we need to know. . . . Other things could
maybe hurt us even more, so we made the decision
not to write for the [court] documents.

Tom, nothing need ever be said to us regarding
Diane. To our way of thinking, this would be a
matter strictly between you and God. And He is so
ready to completely forgive you and *forget* even that
you have sinned against Him. . . . How I pray that
this will become reality for you.

The Visit

The pounding rain matched the pounding of my heart as we
dashed into the prison. We made our way through the visitors'
entrance and we were faced with the necessity of being
examined. Were we carrying any weapons? Anything harmful
at all?

We deposited everything—wallets, watches, and our coats—
in a locker. We discovered the security staff had been alerted to
watch for our coming because of the unusual nature of our
visit.

As we sat in the private interview room which the chaplain
had arranged for us, my heart pounded. We had no intention of
doing anything spectacular, or noble, or unique. Rather, it was

to be a simple personal visit . . . a mission of love. But as I sat there, the magnitude of what was actually taking place hit me full force. We were about to face the person by whose hands our precious daughter's life had been taken. I lifted a quick prayer to God for this unusual moment.

I pushed the feeling of apprehension from me. As early as 1976 the subject of some day meeting with Tom had come up in our letters. We had spent 12 months planning for this moment. Once we knew we would be visiting friends and vacationing in California, we decided to place our special friend on the agenda. And he agreed. We had made all the proper arrangements with the prison chaplain and prison authorities. The chaplain and his assistant were waiting with us at that moment should we need their help or guidance.

The door opened; Tom entered the room. He was about 6 feet tall, dark-haired and muscular, cleanly dressed and shaven . . . a person. God's love welled up within me and overflowed. Tom paused, his eyes filling with tears. My husband and I stood and each in turn embraced Tom. We wept together. Standing by, the chaplain wept openly. Afterward, he said our meeting reminded him of parents receiving their long lost son.

God made us comfortable with one another and we talked for over three hours. We shared our lives and our families and yes, our faith in God. We told him how wonderfully gracious God had been in sustaining us through our difficult days and then rewarding us by placing forgiveness for him within us.

Several times Tom told us he had not intended to kill Diane. He would start to relate the events of that evening, and each time we would say, "Tom, we've not come here to ask you to dig up the past. We're interested in you as a person today. God can make you into a new creation." To this day, there are many details about the rape and murder that we do not know, nor do we desire to know.

Through the help of the chaplain and Tom, arrangements were made for us to share with a gathering of about 70 inmates in the chapel. We told them of God's tremendous miracle of forgiveness in our hearts and the offer of forgiveness for them through Jesus Christ. Some of those hardened criminals sat there listening and were touched, blowing their noses and wiping their eyes.

Despite our joy in seeing Tom and sharing with some of his friends, one thing marred our visit. News reporters had discovered that Bob and I were meeting with Tom. One newspaper printed front page stories of our visit for several days straight. The story was picked up by one of the wire services and carried in newspapers across the country with headlines such as: "Couple visit jailed rapist who killed their daughter," "Mother to face her daughter's killer," and "Pair hugs daughter's murderer."

The publicity was intense, unwanted, and at times untruthful. We had not, as several reports claimed, made a special pilgrimage to forgive. Our forgiveness of Tom had been immediate. The miracle of forgiveness for our daughter's killer took place long before he had been apprehended.

Reporters attended the meeting held in the chapel. We tried to ignore them, though their presence bothered me. To avoid the reporters at the end of the meeting, prison officials ushered us out of the chapel before the last hymn ended. Tom seemed reluctant to have us leave. He hugged us once more.

One of the last statements he made was, "I am not yet born again. I can see it is a tremendous commitment to make and when I make it, I want it to be genuine. I am not ready to make such an important decision. Please keep praying for me."

Three months after we returned home, we received our last letter from Tom. He said he no longer desired to correspond with us. The publicity generated by our visit had offended him.

I could hardly get through the letter without the tears falling. I prayed, with a questioning and hurting heart. "Oh God, how did we fail?"

Often non-Christians expect perfection from those who are born again. We often are not allowed to be the human beings we truly are, subject to all kinds of failures, mistakes, and sins.

Had our friend discovered a flaw in our Christianity?

As I thought about the situation, read God's Word and talked with Him, I began to see that subconsciously, I really wanted to be in on "the act" when God saved Tom. Why else had he been brought into our lives in such a dramatic way? How selfish and thoughtless I had been! Of course God would save him, but He didn't need me in on it. I had made my contribution, perhaps. God was fully able to go on from there, completing the work He had begun in this special life. He didn't need me.

I was willing to let God handle it in His way. It took me awhile to reach that point. I had hung on, reluctant to let go, without really realizing this was how I felt. In surrendering Tom to Christ, I was free again. I knew Tom was in God's hands. I could trust God completely.

I wrote Tom one last letter:

It never so much as entered our minds to seek publicity. . . . However, once the news was out . . . it was out for all to read, then I guess we thought we had all agreed to accept it and to make the best of it, let God use it for something good, if He would.

Bob's and my subsequent actions were done with good intentions, not realizing we would be adding hurt to hurt. We were thoughtless . . . and we are sorry. . . .

You have reason now to distrust us and question our intentions, perhaps even our Christian faith. We have made errors in judgment, but they were honest human errors . . . never with the thought of making things difficult for you in any way. We are not perfect . . . because people are imperfect. Jesus Christ is the only One who will never be a disappointment.

I still pray for Tom every day, knowing that God can continue to work in his life. I may be wrong, but I feel that when he *does* receive Christ, we will be among the first to know.

But my story doesn't end there. Diane's death brought me face to face with the necessity of forgiving others. It's not that I hadn't ever forgiven before; it's not that the concept of forgiveness was foreign to me. I just hadn't given the idea much thought or study before her death. And of course I hadn't been faced with forgiving something of such magnitude.

Once we had forgiven Diane's killer, and particularly after some people began to disapprove of our actions, I searched the Scriptures to see what God had to say about the subject. Through my study, and in talking with people, I've discovered before we can extend true forgiveness to others, we must be forgiven ourselves. Receiving God's forgiveness through Jesus Christ is the foundation on which we build a forgiving lifestyle.

2
Forgiveness: Man's Greatest Need

The Lord our God is merciful and forgiving, even though we have rebelled against Him (Dan. 9:9).

"In my work in therapy," says Dr. Richard P. Walters, staff psychologist at the Pine Rest Christian Hospital in Grand Rapids, Michigan, "I have not seen people have much success in forgiving others apart from incorporating the assistance of their spiritual faith into the process. On the other hand, I've seen some rather astonishing therapeutic outcomes in situations involving people with an active religious faith."

Faith in Christ—that's the foundation for a forgiving lifestyle. In construction as well as life, foundations are important. If a house is built on sand, it will fall when a great storm hits (Matt. 7:26-27). If our value system is based on the shifting sand of fashion, on whatever philosophy is currently "in," like the house, we too run the risk of falling when the storms of life hit. If we are serious about wanting to forgive, we must check to see if our foundation is secure.

Laying My Foundation
It was Valentine's Day. Like many 14-year-old girls, I was preparing to give my heart away. But unlike many other girls, I

was preparing to give my heart to Jesus.

I was a minister's daughter. From the time I was very young, I was immersed in an atmosphere of Christianity, Christian values, and biblical beliefs. I had been baptized as a baby, gone to Sunday School and church since age three weeks, and had always been a "good" girl. Because of all this, I could have grown up believing I already was a Christian. But my parents, being faithful to God's Word, taught each of us children that we must individually receive Christ and that personal forgiveness of sin was the greatest of all our needs.

So on Valentine's Day, during an evangelistic campaign, I responded to the prompting of the Holy Spirit and went forward at the close of my father's message. Kneeling there at the altar, I prayed to receive Christ as my Saviour and my sins were forgiven. Forgiven completely, and forgotten. Forever!

From all outward appearances, this was not a demonstrative event. But I knew, within, I had become a "new creation" in Christ Jesus. The old had gone, the new had come (2 Cor. 5:17). I was aware I could have made this decision right where I was seated in church, or back home in the privacy of my bedroom, or during my walk to school. There was no particular merit in going forward publicly. The response to Christ entering my life would have been the same no matter where I might have been. But it seemed right, as the Holy Spirit was convicting and drawing me, to walk down the aisle of my father's church and place my trust eternally in Jesus Christ. I believe if I had not made that decision to receive Christ, and if I had not grown in my relationship with Him in the following years, I probably would not have been able to forgive Diane's murderer.

It's Not a Religion

I learned early in life that Christianity is anchored in Jesus Christ. He is the foundation on which we build (1 Cor. 3:11). "Salvation is found in no one else, for there is no other name under heaven given to men by which we must be saved" (Acts 4:12).

Religions and cults of the world, be they Eastern mysticism, Buddhism, Islam, Mormonism, or the ones more recently brought to the fore, such as the Unification Church, Scientology, The Way, Humanism, or even Jim Jones' People's Temple, do not build their framework on belief in Jesus Christ. In each of these religions, mankind tries reaching up to God or a god. But Christianity is our gracious God lovingly reaching down to all of us in the person of His Son, Jesus Christ. Christianity is a personal relationship with Jesus Christ which begins the moment we receive Him as our Saviour.

Accepting Christ, being born again, saved, converted, born from above, spiritually reborn, forgiven—whatever the name —is so simple that even young children can understand and accept the concept. Yet it is so mind-boggling that many educated men and women cannot fathom it. If Christ is a liar, a lunatic, or just another fine human teacher, then Christianity fails. But if Christ is who He says He is—the Son of God, our Saviour, our only means to God and eternal life—we need to pay attention to His message.

His Message Is Forgiveness

Forgiveness was very much a part of Jesus' lifestyle. He forgave the paralytic (Matt. 9:2), the sinful woman (Luke 7:47), the woman caught in adultery (John 8:10-11)—even the men who nailed Him to the cross (Luke 23:34). In fact, Jesus' whole purpose in coming to earth was to die so that our sins could be forgiven. Accepting this great divine forgiveness enables us to forgive others.

To forgive someone or something implies that a wrong has been done. What wrong have we done? Jesus said:

What comes out of a man is what makes him unclean. For from within, out of men's hearts, come evil thoughts, sexual immorality, theft, murder, adultery, greed, malice, deceit, lewdness, envy, slander, arrogance, and folly. All these evils come from inside and make a man unclean (Mark 7:20-23).

No amount of ritual, self-discipline, or change of environment can make us clean and acceptable with God. Our problem is a failure to live up to God's standard. The Bible calls it sin. Sin entered the world in the Garden of Eden. Adam and Eve's rebellion against God, called the Fall of man, caused sin to enter the world (Rom. 5:12).

All God's laws were given to show us how we would have to live to earn our salvation. When we measure our own lives against these verses, we see areas in which we've failed. Even if we kept all the laws, but broke one—that wouldn't be good enough for God (James 2:10). God's standard is perfection.

Let me illustrate this idea. If Olympic gold medalist Mark Spitz and an average swimmer tried to swim from California to Hawaii, who would reach Hawaii first? The answer, of course, is that neither one of them would. The average swimmer might swim out a quarter mile or so, and Spitz might double or triple that distance. But neither would make it to Hawaii because the distance is too great. Similarly, the distance between man in his imperfection and God in His holiness is too great for any man to cross. From our perspective one man might be better than another, but no man ever reaches the goal—perfection.

Because we cannot be perfect, even our "good" actions are not good enough to win God's favor. This fact bothers many people who are depending on their well-spent lives to get them to heaven. "All our righteous acts are like filthy rags" (Isa. 64:6). No one is exempt. "But the Scripture declares that the whole world is a prisoner of sin" (Gal. 3:22).

Our Conscience Warns Us

I met a man in prison whom many have read about. His name is Charles "Tex" Watson. He is now one of God's redeemed and forgiven children, a beautiful witness to God's love and forgiving grace. But this was not always true in Tex Watson's life. He had some heavy guilt to deal with, a conscience not clear before God. And for a very good reason. While under the influence of drugs, he had murdered seven people.

As I write this chapter, the movie "Jesus" is premiering in several Michigan cities. One of its actors, Andy Hill, told my co-author Carol McGinnis that after one of the scenes was filmed, two of the actors portraying disciples approached the one playing Jesus. They asked him if he thought God would forgive them for the men they had killed during the Six Day War. Like Tex Watson, they felt guilty.

Each one of us feels guilt over some of our actions and thoughts. A minister uses this fact when presenting the plan of salvation. When a person declares, "I am not a sinner," the minister asks, "Have you ever done or said anything you later regretted?" Often the response is, "But how did *you* know?"

When we break one of God's laws, we set off our inner alarm—the conscience. The conscience often causes us to feel guilty before God and man.

Psychologists and psychiatrists tell us that there are two types of guilt: guilt over specific wrong actions, and a deeper all pervasive guilt over what we are. To deal with guilt, many world religions teach their followers to pay penance or make amends for their wrong conduct. Dr. Charles W. Keysor in his book *Come Clean* writes, "We are all stained and corroded with guilt for being less than God intends us to be. This is why we so often feel unclean . . . hostile . . . alienated" (Victor Books, p. 18).

Verdict: Guilty

God's penalty for sin is death. This is the penalty Tex Watson faced. It is the same penalty we all face without Christ.

There are three expressions of this death penalty. We were created with three distinct parts—the body or physical being; the soul, which consists of the mind, will, and emotions; and the spirit, the non-material part designed to communicate with God. When Adam and Eve disobeyed God, their spirits died immediately. They could no longer communicate with God. Later they experienced physical death.

Since that time, we are all born with dead spirits. We die

physically, and those who don't receive God's provision for a pardon, experience eternal death. This is eternal separation from God. "For the wages of sin is death, but the gift of God is eternal life in Christ Jesus our Lord" (Rom. 6:23).

God's Provision

But our loving God doesn't leave us hanging, hopelessly awaiting a death penalty. He devised a way for us to escape the punishment for sin. This is the Gospel, the Good News found in the Bible.

When Adam and Eve first disobeyed, God killed animals and used their skins to provide Adam and Eve a covering (Gen. 3:21). That established the pattern of an innocent substitute of God's choosing, shedding its blood for sin.

Later, God instructed Moses in a system of animal sacrifices to atone for sin. Every time a person sinned, a sacrifice had to be offered; once a year, year after year, the whole Jewish nation offered a sacrifice. Each sacrifice only covered sin temporarily. "The Law is only a shadow of the good things that are coming—not the realities themselves" (Heb. 10:1). In other words, the animal sacrifices were only pictures of the once-for-all sacrifice that was to come. Isaiah described this once-for-all sacrifice:

He was despised and rejected by men, a man of sorrows and familiar with sufferings. . . . He was pierced for our transgressions, He was crushed for our iniquities; the punishment that brought us peace was upon Him, and by His wounds we are healed. . . . and the Lord has laid on Him the iniquity of us all. He was oppressed and afflicted, yet He did not open His mouth; He was led like a lamb to the slaughter, and as a sheep before her shearers is silent, so He did not open His mouth (Isa. 53:3, 5-7).

Who was this man of sorrows, our perfect sacrifice? Jesus Christ! That is why John the Baptist called Jesus, "The Lamb of God, who takes away the sin of the world" (John 1:29).

Tex Watson received this Lamb of God, and all his sins—even his inhuman acts—were washed away. Tex now says, as overwhelmed with remorse as he is for his own criminal record, he is so grateful for the truth that God, through Christ, has actually provided a covering for his ugly crimes by forgiving them. He has forgiven and forgotten that they ever took place. People can't, but God has! And because of Christ, Tex is a free man inside prison walls.

Was Jesus the Real Messiah?

While John the Baptist was in jail he sent two disciples to ask Jesus:

Are You the One who was to come, or should we expect someone else?

Jesus replied, "Go back and report to John what you hear and see: the blind receive sight, and lame walk, those who have leprosy are cured, the deaf hear, the dead are raised, and the Good News is preached to the poor" (Matt. 11:3-5).

Jesus had quoted from the Old Testament which predicted the Messiah would perform acts of mercy. Jesus fulfilled many of the Old Testament prophecies concerning the Messiah.

Isaiah predicted that the Messiah would be born of a virgin (Isa. 7:14); Matthew recorded that Jesus *was* born of a virgin (Matt. 1:18-23). To the natural mind this is ridiculous, but "all things are possible with God" (Mark 10:27).

Micah predicted the Messiah would be born in Bethlehem (Micah 5:2, 4-5); Matthew recorded that Jesus *was* born in Bethlehem (Matt. 2:4-6). God had arranged Mary's pregnancy to coincide with her and Joseph's journey to Bethlehem to pay taxes.

Zechariah predicted the Messiah would be betrayed for 30 pieces of silver (Zech. 11:12); Matthew recorded that Judas Iscariot *did betray* Jesus for that exact amount of money (Matt. 26:14-15).

Hal Lindsey, an expert in Bible prophecy, has written that

nearly 300 Old Testament prophecies concerning the coming Messiah were literally fulfilled in the birth, life, and death of Jesus Christ *(The Liberation of Planet Earth,* Zondervan, p. 78*).* But there's more.

Jesus Himself believed He was the Messiah. He asked His disciples who people thought He was. They said that some called Him John the Baptist, others thought He might be Elijah, and still others, Jeremiah or one of the prophets.

"But what about you?" He asked, "Who do you say that I am?"

Simon Peter answered, "You are the Christ, the Son of the living God."

Jesus replied, "Blessed are you, Simon son of Jonah, for this was not revealed to you by man, but by My Father in heaven" (Matt. 16:15-17).

Jesus agreed with Peter that He was the Son of God. He claimed to be both God and man. As a Man, He ate (Matt. 26:26), He slept (Luke 8:23), He cried (John 11:35), He became angry (Mark 11:15-17). As God, He accepted worship and He forgave sins (Matt. 9:1-8; 14:33; Mark 2:2-12; John 4:24-26; Acts 10:43).

Can we know God without knowing His Son? It's impossible. Some people will have nothing to do with Jesus Christ, yet they are constantly reaching up to and praying to Jehovah God. This doesn't work, for Jesus and His Father are one (John 10:30; 17:22).

Christ's life—including His many miraculous works, His death, and His resurrection—are all evidences of His validity. Many have tried to explain away His resurrection by saying Christ only fainted on the cross. But the Bible records He had been mercilessly beaten and weakened from lack of sleep, food, and water before He was nailed to the cross. Crucifixion was one of the cruelest forms of punishment; it was designed to kill its victims slowly. Roman soldiers, who would have gained nothing by lying, said that Jesus was dead. In the face of all this, could He only have fainted?

Only Christ claimed He would rise again from the grave, and live. He did! Confucius, Buddha, Mohammed and all other religious leaders are still in their graves. Christ also made numerous appearances after He rose from the grave, giving further proof of His resurrection. The Bible records 11 such appearances before He ascended to heaven to be with His Father again. (See Matt. 28:8-10, 16-20; Mark 16: 12-13; Luke 24:34; John 20:11-18, 19-23, 24-29; 21:1-24; Acts 1:9-11; 1 Cor. 15: 6, 7.) One appearance was before 500 people.

Born Again? How?

Since the 1976 presidential campaign when Jimmy Carter announced he had been born again, there has been a barrage of born again people and products. The term crops up often. Unfortunately, its continued usage has clouded its real meaning. People today wonder what it really means to be born again.

This is not a new term—it is a biblical phrase. "Yet to all who received Him, to those who believed in His name, He gave the right to become children of God—children born not of natural descent, nor of human decision or a husband's will, but born of God" (John 1:12-13). Jesus said to Nicodemus, "I tell you the truth, unless a man is born again, he cannot see the kingdom of God" (3:3).

As we are born into the natural world and become members of our human families, so we must be born into the spiritual world to become members of God's family. We must believe that Christ is who He claims to be, and that by dying on the cross, Christ accepted the punishment we deserved. His death was the greatest and most loving act of forgiveness of all time.

God our Father suffered unspeakably, for He dealt that horrible death blow to His one and only Son. As He was dying, Jesus was totally pressed down with the load of our evil. It temporarily separated Him from His dearest One—for God, in His holiness and perfection, cannot look upon sin.

God's Son suffered unspeakably, for He was spotless—

without sin—yet He carried all of our sin within His own body on Calvary. He took our punishment as though He deserved it. His blood literally paid our ransom fee, absorbed our guilt, and set us free!

Joe Mason, director of Prison Mission Association of Riverside, California was holding regular weekly meetings in a prison with little visible response. Henry Gonzales, nicknamed Gonzy, had been sentenced for 150 years for murdering the chief of police in a New Mexico city. One evening when Mr. Mason and his colleagues were holding a chapel service, Gonzy slipped into the back row. Up till then, he had only ridiculed this group of men and what they were doing. He not only heard the Gospel story, but he listened. Afterward, one of the Christian workers approached Gonzy and asked, "Why don't you receive Christ tonight?"

"I can't," Gonzy replied. "I've read in the Bible that there won't be any murderers in heaven. No murderer inherits eternal life. There just isn't any hope for someone like me."

The Christian worker replied, "But Gonzy, the Bible also says that Christ has paid your penalty, the price for your sin! When you take Him as your Saviour, then He becomes the murderer for you."

Gonzy had never heard it said like that before. He could hardly believe those wonderful hope-giving, life-giving words. "Christ becomes the murderer and I go free? Free, finally, of this load of guilt I've dragged around for so many years?" he asked.

This hardened murderer, who later admitted to killing three men, two of them after his incarceration, stood up. With tears in his eyes, he headed toward the front of the chapel. And, wonder of wonders, 17 other men followed him.

The speaker, seeing this tremendous response, went over the plan of salvation again as simply and carefully as he could. He wanted to be sure those men understood what they were doing. Then Gonzy and the 17 other men received Christ.

Christ made a new man out of Gonzy; he began studying his

Bible, witnessing, and preaching. Many of his fellow inmates became Christians because Gonzy had been made alive in his spirit. Recognizing the positive change in Gonzy, the state granted him a lifetime parole three years after his conversion. Still later he was given a full pardon. He has served his Christ faithfully from that time on.

It is impossible for us to fully comprehend the fact that whatever we have done or been, Christ became on the cross. He literally paid our penalty. Because of this truth, we too along with Gonzy can say, "I am freed from this terrible guilt; I am forgiven! What a blessed relief!" (See Ps. 32:1)

Clothes of Righteousness

When we receive Christ our sins are washed away and we're given a new position before God. God declares us righteous (2 Cor. 5:21; Phil. 3:8-9). We cannot become righteous through our own efforts. God's standard is much too high. So it is important to allow God to dress us with his robe of righteousness to meet His perfect standard (Isa. 61:10). Then God, in His love, sees us through Jesus Christ as perfect sons and daughters. Perfect not because of our perfection, but rather because we have taken on the Son's perfection—and by doing this have met God's perfect standard.

What Will You Do?

Jesus clearly stated, "I am the way and the truth and the life. No one comes to the Father except through Me" (John 14:6). Today, many people believe and teach that one way to God is as good as another and that all religious roads ultimately lead to God. We are deceiving ourselves because Jesus is the only way. "There is a way that seems right to a man, but in the end it leads to death" (Prov. 14:12).

This may seem harsh and narrow-minded to some, but it was the only fair method God could adopt. Had He based salvation on wealth, good deeds, intelligence, good looks, nationality— on anything other than simple childlike faith—He would have been favoring certain groups of people. Since God doesn't discriminate, He devised only one way to heaven—a way that could be easily understood and that would cut across social and cultural barriers. That way is Jesus Christ.

If you have not had an encounter with Christ, do so right now. Jesus said, "Here I am! I stand at the door and knock. If anyone hears My voice and opens the door, I will come in and eat with him, and he with Me" (Rev. 3:20)

He is waiting to be invited in. Being a gentleman, He will not crash into your life nor coerce you into receiving Him. The door to your heart must be opened voluntarily. This can be done by praying a simple prayer: *Dear Father, I admit I am a sinner. I believe the Lord Jesus Christ died for me. I trust Jesus Christ to forgive my sins right now. Let me start a new and meaningful life with You today. Amen.* He will do just that. Count on it!

It's the First Step

Whether you have just decided to follow Christ or have been His child for years, your foundation for a forgiving lifestyle has been laid. Christ gives us the motivation to forgive and He gives us the power to forgive. Do we know Christ? If so, then we are ready to go on.

For further study on the birth and grounding in the Christian faith, the authors recommend: *How to be Born Again* by Billy Graham (Word Books); *The Liberation of Planet Earth* by Hal Lindsey (Zondervan); *Mere Christianity* by C.S. Lewis (MacMillian Publishing Co.); *Yet Will I Trust Him* by Peg Rankin (Regal Books).

3
Just What Is Forgiveness?

Nobody should seek his own good, but the good of others (1 Cor. 10:24).

Our neighbor ran over from next door. Baffled, she sharply asked, "Why aren't you on your way to California to hunt down that maniac-murderer, and rip him limb from limb?"

Bob, the boys, and I looked at one another and then at our neighbor. Just hours before, we had learned of Diane's death, but the idea of seeking revenge had not occurred to us. This was our first indication we were reacting unusually—at least, compared with what society expected.

Word seemed to spread quickly that our family held no bitterness toward Diane's killer; people wanted to know why. In the fall of 1971, I spoke for the first time at a retreat, presenting the story of Diane's life and death and the miracle of forgiveness in our lives. Since that time, I have spoken to church groups, women's seminars, retreats, and fellowships throughout Michigan, Indiana, Ohio, Illinois, and Ontario.

Without exception, one or more people will come to me after I've finished speaking, saying they have great difficulties in forgiving. They openly confess it. For the most part, these are

Christian people admitting they cannot forgive.

After speaking in a church in Michigan, a Christian man approached me and said, "I admire you for what you have done, but I couldn't do it, and furthermore, I wouldn't do it." For reasons I have never been sure of, a pastor I know removed my first book from his church library. I can only wonder if forgiveness has become a neglected message in our pulpits.

Society, both Christian and non-Christian, has somehow become geared to seek revenge. Forgiveness is not the norm. After our visit with Tom, and then the publication of my first book, we received numerous letters, many of them from people who could not understand what we had done or why we had done it.

One 75-year-old woman went so far as to call our visit "one of the most atrocious, unforgivable acts I have ever heard of hidden under the guise of Christianity." She went on to accuse us of hating our daughter and planning her death.

At 2 A.M. one morning a nurse from Canada called. Fifteen years before, she had been raped. She was very disturbed to learn we had forgiven a man who had raped our daughter. "You did a terrible thing," she shouted. "Those beasts should never be released. They should be put away with a needle. I wouldn't hesitate to do it." She hung up before my husband Bob could respond.

Forgiveness is uncommon. This may be because we really don't understand what forgiveness is and therefore, don't know how to give it. The dictionary gives a simple definition of forgiveness: the willingness to forgive. To forgive is to: (1) grant a pardon for something or to someone; (2) cease to blame or feel resentment about an offense or offender; or (3) cancel or let off a debt. For Christians the purpose of forgiveness is three fold: (1) to restore or create a relationship between two people; (2) to promote unity in the body of Christ; and (3) to demonstrate to the world the powerful forgiving love of Jesus Christ.

Practically speaking, what is forgiveness?

Forgiveness Is Not Natural

We all make mistakes, but for some reason we have problems forgiving the mistakes of others. Part of the problem is that forgiving others is not our natural reaction. Forgiveness is a supernatural action. To attempt to truly forgive another without relying on God's strength is improbable. If we are going to extend forgiveness, we must overcome the roadblocks of pride, fear, revenge, and social pressure.

Many hurts we experience come from those we love the most—our family, friends, and neighbors. They may say something unkind to us or about us; they snub us. They forget our birthdays or wedding anniversaries; or they don't invite us to their parties. In these cases we may find it difficult to forgive because our pride has been wounded.

In our society pride has come to mean several things, such as self-respect or satisfaction in a job well-done. This appreciation for excellence is not detrimental. But there is a pride that can hinder us from forgiving another. This perverted pride distorts our vision. It is the source of self-centeredness. When we think of ourselves as all important, we tend to take offense at slights, to be resentful toward others. Paul warns, "Do not think of yourself more highly than you ought, but rather think of yourself with sober judgment" (Rom. 12:3).

In more serious offenses such as violent crimes, divorce, and slander, the roadblock to forgiveness is our natural desire for revenge. When we're hurt, we want to fight back; we want to take justice into our own hands. Given the right circumstances, we *all* are capable of being very hostile toward others.

We may fear that our forgiveness puts a stamp of approval on the other person's actions; that it gives the person who hurt us a license to hurt us again and again. Extending forgiveness makes us vulnerable and we fear that. We may also fear our forgiving actions will be misunderstood.

If we are afraid to take the risk of being misunderstood, we will not forgive. Some people think that if you tell lies about me and I forgive you, the lies must be true. Or if you and I fight and

I apologize first, I must have been the one in the wrong (Doris Donnelly, *Learning to Forgive,* MacMillan Publishing Co., p. 28). One Christian lady told me her husband had shot her and because she could and did forgive him, her Christian friends thought she was crazy. I imagine many thought she had somehow been responsible for his assault.

In our society a forgiving person is viewed as weak, soft, or terribly misguided. Society says that certain people don't deserve forgiveness. Doris Donnelly, in her book *Learning to Forgive,* cites America's prison system as an example of this attitude.

> There are always groups of persons who fall beyond the pale of the restorative practice of forgiveness. Persons who are not dealt with forgivingly are dealt with punitively. Once we deal punitively, we cancel the possibility for forgiveness.
>
> Our prison system, as everyone knows, operates within the punitive model—not the forgiving model of "rehabilitation, restoration, and reintegration into society," and maybe that's why so few of these things ever get done. Convicts never know forgiveness; instead—if they are lucky—they may know conditional pardons and paroles (p. 19).

She continues, "When we are able to perceive people as nonpeople, as objects who don't matter, then we don't have to worry about forgiving" (p. 23).

Calvin Goddard, who works in public relations for the Michigan Department of Corrections, says, "If it is in our capacity as human beings to believe that change is possible, if we are able to allow a person the opportunity to give back a part of what he has taken away, if we ourselves can forget long enough to forgive, then we, as a society, not the offender, will be the ones who will benefit."

Society as a whole is not geared in this direction. We are a cruel people, impatient, cranky, very hostile. As Christians, unforgiving attitudes should not characterize our lives, but often they do. After hearing me speak in Michigan, a woman in her early 30s told me her dad had been murdered a few years before. As a Christian she had just about reached the point where she could forgive the man who committed the murder, but to *pray* for him? It had never entered her mind. Had he only been an object to her? She was now going to begin to pray that God would touch his soul for eternity.

Several persons said it was a revelation to them when I mentioned that as Diane's assailant entered the visitors' room at the prison, I realized he was a *person*. A person made in God's image, created to have fellowship with Him, and with a soul as valuable to God as my own. This perspective helped some people see that criminals are persons with immortal souls whom God loves . . . *real people*. They are not objects to be disregarded and thought of as animals. Rather they are persons whom God says we should love and forgive. There are no people God cannot or will not forgive. And if He forgives, how can we do any less?

Forgiveness Costs

Any time we forgive, whether the offense is petty or serious, we are consenting to be wronged. We give up our rights and that is always costly. It hurts. We agree to bear the pain of the other person's wrong action. "But the loss we shall sustain is but a trifle compared to that vast loss that Jesus suffered to forgive us," says author Roy Hession ("You Must Forgive," *Moody Monthly,* May 1977, p. 54). Whenever we wonder if it will cost us too much to forgive, we should look at Christ's example.

The cost of Christ's forgiveness began when He decided to come to earth. Christ, co-existent with the Father from eternity, chose to set aside His glory, to set aside equality with the Father and be confined in a human body—a body that would tire, hurt, and bleed.

Christ was born into a humble family and no doubt was deprived of material possessions. It was hardly the type of lifestyle the world would expect of the Son of God. Because of the supernatural circumstances surrounding His conception, He was branded illegitimate by some. He was misunderstood by His family, and once He began His public ministry, He was hounded and mocked. He had no place "to lay His head" (Matt. 8:20). He depended on His heavenly Father to provide, through His followers, His food and lodging.

Christ was betrayed by a man He had counted among His friends. Roman soldiers tracked Him down and arrested Him in the middle of the night. "The proper manner, taught by the academy of soldiery in Rome, was to take the victim by the right wrist, twist his arm behind him so that his knuckles touched between his shoulder blades and, at the same time, jam the heel down on his right instep. This was the beginning of the pain . . ." (Jim Bishop, *The Day Christ Died,* Pocket Books, Inc., pp. 227-228).

The pain continued throughout the night. With His arms bound behind Him and a noose around His neck, Jesus was first taken before Caiaphas, the high priest, and all the elders and teachers of the law. There He was falsely accused. "Then they spit in His face and struck Him with their fists. Others slapped Him and said, 'Prophesy to us, Christ. Who hit You?'" (Matt. 26:67-68).

Early the next morning the chief priests and elders decided to take Jesus to the governor Pilate for trial. Pilate sent Jesus to Herod. "Then Herod and his soldiers ridiculed and mocked Him. Dressing Him in an elegant robe, they sent Him back to Pilate" (Luke 23:11). By then Christ had been standing many hours; He had no food or sleep.

Pilate buckled under public pressure and ordered that Jesus be flogged and then crucified. The flogging was most likely done with a short, circular piece of wood with several strips of leather attached. At the end of each strip of leather was a chunk of bone or piece of iron. The flogging or scourging was called the "halfway death" because it was supposed to stop this side of death (Jim Bishop, *The Day Christ Died,* p. 302).

Then they took Jesus away to crucify Him. "They offered

Him wine to drink, mixed with gall," a sort of anesthetic, but Jesus refused it (Matt. 27:34). Jesus felt each nail as it was driven through His wrists. He felt the soldiers nail His right foot over His left.

He suffered pain from the nail wounds. He had muscle cramps in His forearms, upper arms, legs, and thighs. When He let His body sag, He could not breath.

Throughout this intense pain and suffering, people mocked and scorned Him. "Come down from the cross, if You are the Son of God!" (v. 40) Soldiers gambled for His clothes; people gaped at His wounds.

Jesus had had no food or water for 14 hours. He was thirsty, tired, hungry, dizzy, feverish, but above all—in pain. After hanging on the cross 3 hours, He died.

The agonizing suffering for sin and the separation from His heavenly Father only compounds the cost to Christ for our forgiveness. We will never be able to really understand the depths of His suffering for bearing our sin. That was the ultimate!

When we extend forgiveness we may not be giving our lives, but the price can be dear, our suffering intense. It hurts when the extended forgiveness is rejected. I wonder if Tom has rejected our forgiveness. For awhile I was sure he had accepted it; I thought he felt amazed and overwhelmed and yet could not understand it. Chaplain Ray of International Prison Ministry said to me, "When anyone receives forgiveness it is a stark confession that he needs it."

Perhaps Tom doesn't really believe he needs forgiveness. Possibly the injustice of his crime has never really slammed its way into his soul. Maybe he has no remorse. He is a proud young man. He despises the term murderer. I think I can understand that. But though his crime may have been without intent to kill, it *did* happen. We have forgiven, but certainly not without paying a price.

When forgiveness is given and not received, the transaction is incomplete. However, the forgiver has done all he can. If we can be hurt by someone refusing our forgiveness, then how deeply do we hurt God when we refuse His forgiveness toward us?

Yes, forgiving can hurt, especially when our action is misunderstood. I have been accused of being an unnatural mother, extolling my daughter's killer, rather than possessing normal mother love for Diane. While on a local television talk show, Bob and I were asked if we would welcome Tom into our home. My husband said, "Yes, absolutely, that's what forgiveness is all about. We love him." The audience hissed and we hurt. Perhaps some of us anticipate this hurt and shy away from it. The result: we withdraw; we don't expose ourselves; we don't forgive.

Forgiveness Is Not Indifference

After one speaking engagement, two widows approached me. Both of them had been married to police officers who were gunned down in two separate incidents. The women had not been particularly bitter about the incidents; they thought they had forgiven the men responsible for their husbands' deaths. But while listening to me speak, they realized that what they had mistaken for forgiveness was actually indifference. They had chosen to ignore the men involved, perhaps to insulate themselves against the accompanying hurt. They had not even considered that forgiveness should be active; they had not been praying for these men. But they told me they were going to start praying right away.

While at a writer's conference, I talked with two college students about the writing of this book. Both young men agreed that they thought extending forgiveness was important and Christian. However, one of them admitted his indifference toward a man who had raped his girlfriend. He said he tried not to think about the incident or the man.

Trying to keep from thinking about an incident or saying, "Let's forget about it," is not forgiveness. It is indifference. Creath Davis, founder and director of Dallas' Christian

Concern Foundation says that to say, "Let's just forget it," without offering a basis for forgetting is dealing in superficiality. "The result of such action would simply be to bury the problem by blocking it out of the mind," he writes. "At best, any relief would be only temporary" *(How to Win in a Crisis,* Zondervan, p. 23). The basis for forgetting is forgiving. Face the problem, deal with it, and then forget it.

Forgiveness Is Not Agreeing with the Wrong

Many people think that saying, "I forgive you," really means, "I agree with you. What you have done to me is not wrong." But forgiveness is *not* agreeing with the wrong. Forgiveness honestly says, "Yes, you wronged me. I hurt—I hurt a whole lot—but I will not allow that hurt to control me. Instead, by the act of my will, I *will* see you as God does—as an imperfect person in need of forgiveness and love. I will forgive you and with that forgiveness release you of any obligation you may have to repay me."

Christ forgives us this way. He does not agree with our wrongs. He does not pat us on the back and say our sin is OK. When He forgives, He says, "Go, and sin no more" (John 8:11, KJV).

Many times people asked me this question: "Did you want your daughter to die?" Each time I explain: "No, it was sheer agony to lose her." We loved Diane, and certainly, a thousand times over, we would rather have had her remain alive. But the fact is, God chose to allow her death. My responsibility now is to forgive the man who murdered her. It is biblical Christianity.

Scripture nowhere asks us to condone wrong. Sin is sin. The Bible has a standard of right and wrong, and it cannot be changed. Never have we condoned the wrong done to our daughter. It has brought us hurt and anguish. But God has placed love in our hearts for the *person* who did the wrong— not his *action!* We love him not for what he did, but for what God can help him become.

Forgiveness Is an Act of Love

To love someone is to want the best in life for that person. The only way that person can have the best in life is to have Christ, and our forgiveness can be the example that leads that person to receive Christ's forgiveness. There is a saying, "The only Bible some people read is your life." (See 2 Cor. 3:2).

Often the only concept some people have of God is the reflection they see of Christ in our lives. If we are loving and forgiving, people might want to find out more about our Saviour. But if we are cold and calloused, lacking in compassion, people will not want any part of our Lord. If we love people, if we really want them to come to Christ, we will forgive.

Forgiveness Is an Act of the Will

There is no emotional prerequisite for forgiveness. We don't have to *feel* like forgiving before we can forgive. Indeed, our emotions may be pulling us in the opposite direction. Every day we make numerous choices without even thinking about them: What time should I get up? What shall I wear? Where shall I eat lunch?

In the same way, we can deliberately choose to love, to hate, to forgive, or not to forgive. Forgiveness is a matter of the will. Though we may have problems controlling our emotions, we can control our wills. By choosing to forgive, we do ourselves a favor both physically and spiritually.

Forgiveness Is Powerful

Larry Christenson, pastor and author, calls the type of forgiveness we've been discussing "unilateral" forgiveness. In his book *The Renewed Mind* he writes, " 'Unilateral' means 'one-sided.' Unilateral forgiveness is a forgiveness which flows out from the forgiver. The other person does not ask for it, may not even realize he needs it. The forgiver takes the initiative and forgives without waiting for the other person to come and ask for forgiveness." Christenson adds that unilateral forgiveness is "something more powerful than atomic fission. The exercise of that power makes changes for all eternity." The exercise of that power "open[s] the door for God to really deal with a person" (Bethany Fellowship, pp. 53, 60-61).

The power of forgiveness manifests itself in several ways. One is to heal. Evangelist Billy Graham once said that the three most healing words in all the world are, "I forgive you." The healing can be in the spiritual or social realm—establishing or re-establishing a relationship with God or man. The healing can also be physical. There is evidence, both from the Bible and medical authorities, that suggests the person who refuses to forgive can literally make himself ill.

Forgiveness has the power to free both the forgiver and the person causing the offense. God desires that we be free persons in Christ. "So if the Son sets you free, you will be free indeed" (John 8:36). When we hang on to bitterness, resentments, envy, hostility, grudges—any unforgiveness—we become crippled and disabled Christians. We are bound by these unhealthy attitudes, and cannot experience being "free indeed." We are spiritually useless and fruitless.

If I held resentments toward Tom, what would the benefits be for me? I have been told that I have every right to be filled with red hot hate. Yet even if I felt that way, I couldn't touch or harm the one in prison. Revenge would not have brought our precious daughter back. But it would have had a destructive effect on me.

Revenge would have made me a captive in a self-made prison; I would not be free to function in a Christ-honoring fashion. I have known many bitter Christians. Bitterness and happiness cannot be integrated. They cannot both exist in one's heart and that heart remain free.

Forgiveness has freed me and in a sense, I believe my forgiveness has freed Tom—freed him to someday receive Jesus Christ. By cutting us off Tom has tied our hands, at least temporarily, but he hasn't tied God's hands. God is free to work in Tom's heart and life and I am free to pray for Tom, because prayer has no boundaries.

A friend of Carol McGinnis' tells this unusual story:

> For most of my adult life the relationship between my mother and me had been tenuous at best. She was a diagnosed schizophrenic . . . . After particularly nasty incidents at and after her mother's and brother's funerals, I vowed never again to have anything to do with her. But I did keep praying for her salvation and healing.
>
> One morning Mother's friend, Ann, telephoned me to ask if I knew my Aunt Velma, Mother's only living sister, had died. I did.
>
> I again prayed for Mother. My heart began to pound as I read . . . from Matthew 18:21-22: "Then Peter came to Jesus and asked, 'Lord, how many times shall I forgive my brother when he sins against me? Up to seven times?' Jesus answered, 'I tell you, not seven times, but seventy times seven.'"
>
> I bowed my head and whispered, "Thank You, Lord."
>
> I picked up the phone and dialed. Mother's voice, low and weak, answered.
>
> "Mother, is there anything that I can do for you?" I asked.
>
> "I don't want to be alone," she whispered.
>
> "I'll come right away."
>
> I'd like to say that solved all the problems, but it didn't. There was still an eight month period marked with several painful and agonizing incidents. . . .
>
> But I do believe my obedience to God's command that day freed Him to begin healing. At the end of eight months my mother experienced a real miracle that opened her eyes to God's reality and led her to a new commitment, on her own, to Him. Eventually it brought us to a new relationship of love and affection and mutual enjoyment of each other's

company. And God did answer my prayers for her healing and gave us five beautiful years together of friendship and fellowship before taking her home to be with Him. I realize now that my sin of unforgiveness stood in the way of my prayers for her salvation and healing.

This woman had been limiting God's power to work in her mother's life. By not forgiving someone, we may also be preventing God from working in someone's life. Some writers suggest if Stephen, the first martyr, had not forgiven the people responsible for his death, the Apostle Paul might never have had his meeting with Christ.

Forgiveness also has the power to influence others. In 1977, a Virginia newspaper carried a story of a father publicly forgiving the hit-and-run driver who killed his 16-year-old son.

"I learned forgiveness from my son," the father explained. "Now, before God, I want to forgive the person who killed my son . . . . We know if Bobby were still alive, he would be the first to forgive him."

A few years before his death, Bobby had gotten in a fight with one of his friends. His friend knocked out three of his teeth, but even so, the next day Bobby went to his friend and forgave him. This action influenced his father to forgive. Perhaps your act of forgiveness will influence someone else too.

Forgiveness is many things, but most of all, forgiveness is commanded by God. For Christians, forgiveness is not an option.

4

There's No Getting Around God's Commands

> If you love Me, you will obey what I command (John 14:15).

A missionary and his son were playing catch outside their home in a remote South American village. To prove his ability, the 10-year-old took a step away from his father after each throw. Farther and farther away the boy went till he was standing directly under a tree at the edge of some dense growth.

Suddenly becoming serious, the father commanded, "Fall flat on the ground and start crawling toward me."

The boy obeyed instantly.

When he reached his father, the father picked him up and hugged him tightly. The son, somewhat confused, turned to look back at the tree, and there hanging from a limb that had been right above his head was a poisonous snake.

The missionary used this true story to illustrate the reaction we should have to God's commands. Like the little son, we should obey our Father instantly and without question.

A Matter of Perspective

Our concept of God determines our reactions to His commands. If we view Him as angry, mean, a joy-killer, or slave driver, we will see His commands as a burden, as something we are forced to do. We might even think God gives us commands to make us miserable. But if we really believe that God loves us, that He has our best interests in mind, that He gives us commands for our protection and good, we'll view His commands as opportunities to find His best for us.

The missionary's son was secure in his father's love. He obeyed, not because he understood, but because he trusted his father. We can well imagine the consequences if the son had not obeyed. But because he obeyed, instantly and without question, he was protected from very possible harm. Likewise, our unquestioning obedience to God's commands can spare us from spiritual and physical harm.

The basic issue here is this: do we really trust God? If we believe God is all-knowing and all-powerful and He is always in control, do we show our trust by obeying His commands?

A Word About Obedience

Commands are not options from God. We aren't allowed to pick which commands we will follow and which we will ignore. This doesn't mean obedience will come naturally or easily. We question God's commands; we procrastinate; we rebel. We may even try to bargain with God, offering to sacrifice in one area to make up for ignoring a command in another area. But "to obey is better than sacrifice" (1 Sam. 15:22).

Anne Sullivan, the famous teacher of Helen Keller, once said, "I saw clearly that it was useless to try to teach her a language or anything else until she first learned to obey me. I have thought about it a great deal, and the more I review my actions, the more certain I am that obedience is the gateway through which knowledge, yes, and love too, enters the mind of a child" ("Needed: Obedient Children," *Our Daily Bread,* November 28, 1980). So it is with us, God's children.

When we obey God's commands, we live life as God intended it and we receive God's best including love, security, stability, peace, and joy. Dr. Leslie B. Flynn explains: "Doing

God's will is followed by joy. Then joy, in turn, provides strength to obey God's commands. This obedience yields more joy, which again provides the impetus for more submission to the divine will. This continuous, recurring cycle of joy—obedience—joy—obedience makes for a high level of Christian walk" *(The Gift of Joy,* Victor Books, p. 77).

Partial obedience or obedience only when we feel like it does not result in this "high level" walk Dr. Flynn refers to. At best, partial obedience results in frustration and inconsistent spiritual growth. And as far as our feelings are concerned, we may never *feel* like obeying.

Not only does obedience profit us spiritually, it is the only way we can show our love for God. Jesus mentioned this often.

> If you love Me, you will obey what I command. . . . Whoever has My commands and obeys them, he is the one who loves Me. . . . If anyone loves Me, he will obey My teaching. . . . He who does not love Me will not obey My teaching. . . . You are My friends if you do what I command (John 14:15, 21, 23-24; 15:14).

Since obedience is the only way to show God our love, we must obey. Several of God's commands concern forgiveness.

Summing It Up

Jesus commanded us, "Love the Lord your God with all your heart and with all your soul and with all your mind. This is the first and greatest commandment. And the second is like it: Love your neighbor as yourself. All the Law and the prophets hang on these two commandments" (Matt. 22:37-40). "There is no commandment greater than these" (Mark 12:31).

This leaves us no loopholes. Love satisfies the Law of God (Rom. 13:10). Love is the evidence that we're Christ's disciples (John 13:34-35). Love is more than an emotion; it is action—active, down to earth, right now obedience.

To love implies we are to forgive because, after all, forgiveness is sacrificial love for another. Love "is not rude . . . it is not easily angered, it keeps no record of wrongs" (1 Cor.

13:5). Specific commands to forgive are found throughout Scripture. And there are a host of commands on related topics, such as love, mercy, withholding revenge and judgment, and being peacemakers. In fact, the Bible's theme is one of love and forgiveness—forgiveness of man by God and forgiveness of man by man. Try reading through the New Testament sometime and underline each reference to forgiveness and love. These are only a few:

> Love one another deeply, from the heart (1 Peter 1:22).

> Live in peace with each other. . . . Make sure that nobody pays back wrong for wrong, but always try to be kind to each other and to everyone else (1 Thes. 5:13, 15).

> Make every effort to live in peace with all men and to be holy (Heb. 12:14).

> Do not judge, or you too will be judged (Matt. 7:1).

> Bless those who persecute you; bless and do not curse. . . . Live in harmony with one another (Rom. 12:14, 16).

> Be kind and compassionate to one another, forgiving each other, just as in Christ God forgave you. . . . Live a life of love (Eph. 4:32; 5:2).

Tough Questions

Perhaps the best known of the forgiveness commands is found in the Lord's Prayer. Countless people recite this prayer every Sunday in church, but I wonder how many of them pay attention to that phrase: "Forgive us our debts, as we also have forgiven our debtors" (Matt. 6:12). If the person praying has bitterness or hate in his heart, he is praying for God to have bitterness or hate in His heart for him.

Of the seven petitions in the Lord's Prayer, only the one concerning forgiveness is later reemphasized. Christ said, "For if you forgive men when they sin against you, your heavenly Father will also forgive you. But if you do not forgive men their sins, your Father will not forgive your sins" (vv. 14-15). Other verses say, "Do not judge, and you will not be judged. Do not condemn, and you will not be condemned. Forgive, and you will be forgiven. . . . Forgive us our sins, for we also forgive everyone who sins against us" (Luke 6:37; 11:4).

Does God's forgiveness of us hinge on our forgiveness of others? If it does, as these verses seem to imply, doesn't this conflict with the idea that our salvation is based on grace alone? (See Eph. 2:8-9; Gal. 2:16; 3:11; Titus 3:4-7.)

Theologians have explained these verses several ways. "One common explanation seized upon by commentators is to say that these verses simply tell us that a forgiving heart is an evidence of one's salvation" (Wayne Grudem, "Forgiveness: Forever and Today," *His,* February 1980, p. 15). Others say that if our lives are cluttered by unforgiveness, we cannot freely receive God's forgiveness.

Though both these ideas are true, Wayne Grudem goes on to explain:

> We need to realize that the word *forgive* has two different meanings. It can take a *legal* sense and mean "declare someone to be not guilty" or "release someone from the obligation to pay a penalty for breaking the law." That is usually what we mean when we talk about God forgiving our sins.
>
> *Forgive* can have another meaning, however. Sometimes we use it in a more *personal* sense to mean "changing one's attitude toward another person." This is usually the way we use the word *forgive* when talking about human relationships ("Forgiveness: Forever and Today," pp. 15, 28).

I have forgiven my daughter's killer in the *personal* sense. I am not angry with him, or bitter, or resentful. I love him as a son and would welcome him into my home. However, I *have not* and *cannot* forgive him in the *legal* sense. Tom was tried and found guilty under the laws of the state of California. Now he must serve his prison sentence. Only the state has the power to forgive him in the legal sense, to pardon or release him from his obligation to serve out his term. Only God Almighty can forgive Tom in the legal sense for transgressing His law.

Grudem continues:

> Once these two senses of *forgive* are distinguished, Matthew 6:14-15 becomes clearer. We have become so accustomed to thinking about God's forgiving our sins in a legal sense (at conversion) that we assume that Jesus is using *forgive* in a legal sense here.
>
> But Jesus . . . is using it in a personal sense. Although we as Christians have the guilt for our sin removed for all eternity, we still do things that are displeasing to our heavenly Father. . . . We then need to pray, "Forgive us our sins"; that is, "Please do not be displeased with us because of our sins."
>
> We are not asking again for justification . . . or for eternal life with Christ. . . . We are asking for the restoration of a broken relationship ("Forgiveness: Forever and Today," p. 28).

Unforgiveness is sin and a holy God cannot have communion with sin. For this reason, we must daily confess our sins to God.

We Carry a Special Message

As Christians, we have the awesome responsibility of being ambassadors for Christ (2 Cor. 5:20). An ambassador represents another person. We represent Christ and are responsible to proclaim His message of reconciliation to others. For good or bad, our lifestyle is a reflection on our Lord and His message. If we preach love and forgiveness but are filled with hate and bitterness, who will be attracted to our Lord?

"God, in His wisdom, has decided that our forgiving others is so important that when we fail to do so He will disrupt His relationship with us. In this way, we will eventually learn to forgive and love much more" (Wayne Grudem, "Forgiveness: Forever and Today," p. 28).

The Apostle Paul gave specific commands about forgiveness:

> Get rid of all bitterness, rage and anger, brawling and slander, along with every form of malice. Be kind and compassionate to one another, forgiving each other, just as in Christ God forgave you (Eph. 4:31-32).

> Therefore, as God's chosen people, holy and dearly loved, clothe yourselves with compassion, kindness, humility, gentleness, and patience. Bear with each other and forgive whatever grievances you may have against one another. Forgive as the Lord forgave you. And over all these virtues put on love, which binds them all together in perfect unity (Col. 3:12-14).

By practicing forgiveness we will maintain unity in the body of Christ and a vibrant witness for Christ Himself.

Concerning Prayer

Jesus said, "And when you stand praying, if you hold anything against anyone, forgive him, so that your Father in heaven may forgive you your sins" (Matt. 11:25).

R.A. Torrey explained in his classic book *The Power of Prayer,* "Here [Mark 11:25] we are distinctly told that an unforgiving spirit makes it impossible for God to answer our prayers. All of God's answering our prayers is upon the basis of God's dealing with us as forgiven sinners, and God cannot deal with us as forgiven sinners while we are not forgiving those who have wronged us" (Zondervan, pp. 161-162).

Prayer with a forgiving spirit is basic to our spiritual survival; without that forgiving spirit our prayers are useless and our spiritual growth is stunted. (See Ps. 66:18.) Often when I'm out speaking and I mention this, I see raised eyebrows or other surprised looks. I wonder how many people are reviewing their unanswered prayers and checking for an unforgiving spirit. When our prayers go unanswered, we too should check for an unforgiving spirit.

Revenge Is Not an Option

Recently on the front page of the *Detroit Free Press* was a story titled: "Grieving Mother Guns Down Daughter's Killer in Courtroom." A West German woman's 7-year-old daughter had been killed by a man who had been previously convicted of child molesting. During the hearing, the 30-year-old mother opened fire with a pistol in the courtroom and killed the 35-year-old man. The woman was charged with murder *(Detroit Free Press,* March 7, 1981, Section A, p. 1). But what did she accomplish, other than making a bad situation worse?

Revenge is one of the few—perhaps the only—alternative to forgiveness. Yet this option is not open to Christians. "Do not take revenge, my friends, but leave room for God's wrath, for it is written: 'It is mine to avenge: I will repay,' says the Lord" (Rom. 12:19). "Make sure that nobody pays back wrong for wrong, but always try to be kind to each other and to everyone else" (1 Thes. 5:15). "Do not repay evil with evil or insult with insult" (1 Peter 3:9).

Most Christians would not go to the extreme of killing someone, but many believers practice subtle forms of revenge. Some refuse to talk or associate with another; some spread lies and half-truths to destroy another person's character; others get their revenge, though they might not call it that, by being rude to the other person or embarrassing him publicly. Whenever we try to punish someone or hurt him for a wrong done, we are taking revenge and breaking God's command.

How Can We Be So Unfair?

Once while speaking at a Christian Women's Club meeting I explained how I handle the question: How could you forgive a criminal?

I answered, "When I stop to realize how much Christ had to forgive—my terrible debt of sin against Him, one I could never have paid, nor did I deserve to have it paid, yet God, in His unspeakable love for me absorbed my debt in its entirety—how can I not forgive? How dare I withhold forgiveness. Only those of us who have never needed forgiveness dare entertain the thought, *I won't forgive.* And who of us has not needed forgiveness?"

Afterward, a friend approached me. She said, "Goldie, I had not been able to believe that God would call on you to forgive your daughter's killer, but today you made a believer out of me. I can see it now. We must forgive. God, through Christ, has forgiven so very much in my life—how could I even think of not forgiving something of much less significance than my own forgiven debt!"

Jesus illustrated this point with a parable:

Therefore, the kingdom of heaven is like a king who wanted to settle accounts with his servants. As he began the settlement, a man who owed him 10,000 talents was brought to him. Since he was not able to pay, the master ordered that he and his wife and his children and all that he had be sold to repay the debt.

The servant fell on his knees before him. "Be patient with me," he begged, "and I will pay back everything." The servant's master took pity on him, canceled the debt and let him go.

But when that servant went out, he found one of his fellow servants who owed him 100 denarii. He grabbed him and began to choke him. "Pay back what you owe me!" he demanded.

His fellow servant fell to his knees and begged

him, "Be patient with me, and I will pay you back."
But he refused. Instead, he went off and had the man thrown into prison until he could pay the debt. When the other servants saw what had happened, they were greatly distressed and went and told their master everything that had happened.

Then the master called the servant in. "You wicked servant," he said, "I canceled all that debt of yours because you begged me to. Shouldn't you have had mercy on your fellow servant just as I had on you?" In anger his master turned him over to the jailers until he should pay back all he owed.

This is how My heavenly Father will treat each of you unless you forgive your brother from your heart (Matt. 18:23-35).

The king had forgiven a debt of approximately $2 million; the unmerciful servant couldn't even forgive a $20 debt (Warren W. Wiersbe, *Meet Yourself in the Parables,* Victor Books, p. 133). The unmerciful servant offends our sense of fair play, but we're often guilty of this same unfairness. God has forgiven us a tremendous debt; we could never repay Him, even if we became His slaves. But do we always pass on the mercy shown us, or do we act like the unmerciful servant?

Unforgiveness Affects Our Minds and Bodies

So far we have focused on some spiritual reasons why forgiveness is important. But there are other reasons we need to forgive. Notice the last part of the parable of the unmerciful servant (vv. 34-35).

In some versions of the Bible, the word *jailers* in verse 34 is translated as "tormentors" or "torturers." Comments Warren Wiersbe, "This word carries the idea of inner mental torment as much as physical torture" *(Meet Yourself in the Parables,* p. 135). Scripture and medical facts indicate our emotional and . physical well-being are affected when we persist in withholding forgiveness. Unforgiveness can produce bitter fruits in our lives.

5
The Fruit of Unforgiveness

The acts of the sinful nature are obvious: ... hatred, discord, jealousy, fits of rage, selfish ambition, dissensions, factions, and envy. ... But the fruit of the Spirit is love, joy, peace, patience, kindness, goodness, faithfulness, gentleness, and self-control (Gal. 5:19-22).

One Sunday afternoon in 1977 Sandy Jones* was getting into her car with her brother John and her 10-month-old son James. It was a beautiful spring day and the three of them were headed to their church's annual bazaar.

Suddenly an 18-year-old, whom we will call David, crossed the street and came toward them with a knife. He lunged toward Sandy with the knife raised. After a brief scuffle, Sandy escaped his grasp. David then ran around to the other side of the car and through the open window, grabbed the baby's foot.

John struggled to keep hold of James, but David slashed John's arms with the knife, forcing him to release the child. David ran across the street, holding the baby upside down by the ankles.

---

*All of the names in this incident have been changed.

By then, Sandy's husband Ben and her two older sons and several neighbors had come outside and were desperately pleading with David to release the baby to them. David stared blankly at the crowd as he swung the baby back and forth. The crowd continued to plead with David, but he didn't respond. He swung the baby back and forth, back and forth, higher and higher. Finally, he slung the baby to the pavement. Bruised and bleeding, little James was rushed to the hospital where he died.

I first heard this story from Sandy's best friend Jane. Jane wrote to me after she and Sandy saw an article in their local newspaper on Bob's and my visit to Tom's prison. Sandy felt I would understand her reaction to her son's murder, for you see, Sandy had been able to forgive.

Sandy had known the Lord well before this tragedy. Even though her heart was crushed, she realized the only way to deal with this crime and remain free in Christ would be to forgive. She leaned on the Lord, exchanging her hate for His love.

Sandy's husband, however, took an opposing view. Ben threatened to kill David if he ever laid eyes on him again. He became filled with bitterness and hate. Morning, noon, and night Ben's thoughts were occupied with revenge.

Ben took out his hostility on his wife and two older sons by treating them with cruelty and disrespect. He was furious with them for forgiving the baby's killer and spent more and more time away from home, seeking refuge in local taverns. Ben had decided perhaps alcohol would help solve his problems, make him forget his hurt, his hate, his ugly feelings. But drinking was not the answer and Ben began reaping the fruit of unforgiveness. Ben's marriage finally ended in divorce and his intense hatred slowly eroded his personality.

Ben and Sandy's story illustrates dramatically the two paths we can choose to take when faced with an offense. Ben's response toward little James' assailant is much more in keeping with society's attitudes. But unforgiveness doesn't promote physical, emotional, or spiritual well-being. It produces bitter fruit.

Fruit: Good and Bad

The Bible speaks of the fruit of the Spirit. It is love, joy, peace, patience, kindness, goodness, faithfulness, gentleness, and self-control (Gal. 5:22-23). But this fruit doesn't automatically appear in a Christian's life. It flourishes when a believer is totally dependent on Jesus Christ, Holy Spirit controlled, and immersed in the Word of God.

Each Christian has two natures within him: the old and the new. We are born with this old nature, which is often called the flesh or our sinful nature. When we receive Christ, He creates within us the new or spirit nature (2 Cor. 5:17; 1 Cor. 3:16; 6:19).

Paul wrote, "For the sinful nature desires what is contrary to the Spirit, and the Spirit what is contrary to the sinful nature. They are in conflict with each other, so that you do not do what you want" (Gal. 5:17).

What does all this have to do with forgiveness? Forgiveness, I believe, is a spiritual reaction, not a natural reaction. Someone who has not committed his life to Christ will have problems forgiving, and may not even understand why forgiveness is necessary. Some Christians also have problems forgiving. Christians who are not nurturing their spiritual natures through Bible study, prayer and fellowship with other Christians may respond to situations with their old natures. The old nature always says no to unconditional forgiveness.

Christians either produce spiritual fruit or fleshly fruit, but like a tree, we cannot simultaneously produce two types of fruit (Luke 6:43-45; Gal. 6:8). When we forgive we are responding with our spiritual nature and the ultimate result is the fruit of the Spirit. Though the Bible does not call forgiveness a fruit, forgiveness is a facet of love, peace, patience, self-control, and kindness. But when we withhold forgiveness, we reap the fruit of unforgiveness.

The following material on the fruit of unforgiveness is not intended to be a complete list. It's possible I've left out some type of fruit or results of unforgiveness. We must keep in mind that each person is different. When we are unforgiving, we develop different fruit at different rates.

And lastly, some of the fruit can exist in a person's life independent of an unforgiving spirit. Illness is a good example. All sickness is not a result of someone holding a grudge, though holding a grudge often does cause sickness. The same can be said about depression. Or divorce. Or suicide. But if someone is displaying any of this fruit, I challenge that person to examine his life honestly before God. If there is an unforgiving spirit, remove it. Removing unforgiveness is the only thing that frees us of its fruit.

Anger—Top on the List

"Psychologists tell us anger is the instinctive human response to fear, pain, or frustration" (Margie M. Lewis with Gregg Lewis, *The Hurting Parent,* Zondervan, p. 68). With this in mind, it's easy to understand why anger is one of the first emotions we have to deal with when we're faced with a hurt in our lives.

Anger in itself is not wrong. Even the Bible says, "Be ye angry," but with the instruction, "and sin not" (Eph. 4:26, KJV).

We can deal with our anger in three ways: through repression, uncontrolled expression, or controlled expression. Repression and uncontrolled expression are both inappropriate responses and often lie at the root of the other fruit of unforgiveness we will discuss.

Repression ignores the problem for a time, but anger repressed is still anger. It will find expression through another outlet: anxiety, critical attitudes, depression, irritableness, bitterness, distrust, hostility, self-pity, even physical illness. Repression destroys us—bit by bit. However, uncontrolled expression destroys our relationships with others and our credibility as loving and forgiving servants of a loving and forgiving God.

Controlled expression dispels anger and promotes forgiveness and healing. If anger is not dealt with properly, it becomes one of the most dangerous fruits of unforgiveness because it parents many of the other fruits.

Resentment, bitterness, and hostility are all born from anger. Resentment is indignation or displeasure focused at some injustice; it's anger over an injury or hurt.

We often become resentful because we assume that life should be fair. Charles R. Swindoll explains:

> We Americans like things to be logical and fair.... Meaning this: if I do what is right, good will come to me, and if I do what is wrong, bad things will happen to me. Right brings rewards and wrong brings consequences. That's a very logical and fair axiom of life, but . . . it isn't always true *(Improving Your Serve,* Word Books, p. 174).

Life is not fair, nor should we expect it to be. Dr. Jack T. Dean, president of Grace Bible College, suggests Christians should battle resentment by remembering that God is in control (Acts 17:24-25); testings are a gift from God (Phil. 1:29); and the purpose of testing is to produce maturity (James 1:2-4). Despite our trials now, we have a great future awaiting us (1 John 3:2; Rom. 8:18). Our responsibility as believers is to minister, rather than to be ministered to (Mark 10:43-45).

Hanging on to resentment is dangerous. Dan Hamilton writes: "Resentment suppressed will never lose its power; like a spark in a gasoline tank, a bit of momentary friction will set off a devastating explosion" *(Forgiveness,* InterVarsity Press, p. 6). Resentment results in broken friendships, a negative view of life, a loss of energy and efficiency, and psychosomatic illnesses.

Bitterness develops when we dwell on our hurts and injuries, when we refuse to let go of our resentments. The bitter person is often cruel, sarcastic, and filled with hatred and ill will. Bitterness is a cancer which devours the very possibility of love, contentment, or even common sense. "Get rid of all bitterness, rage and anger, brawling and slander, along with every form of malice" (Eph. 4:31).

When the root of bitterness is watered with self-pity and fertilized by dwelling on injustices, it will grow out of proportion, stunting the growth of spiritual fruit and our capacity to love. Says well-known pastor and counselor Tim LaHaye, "I have found that a bitter, unforgiving thought pattern toward someone you hate will even minimize or limit your expressions of love for someone you love" *(How to Win Over Depression,* Zondervan, p. 199).

Reflecting on her experience in a Nazi concentration camp, Corrie ten Boom says, "Those who were able to forgive their former enemies were able to return to the outside world and rebuild their lives, no matter what the physical scars. Those who nursed their bitterness remained invalids. It was as simple and as horrible as that" (Corrie ten Boom with Jamie Buckingham, *Tramp for the Lord,* Revell, pp. 56-57).

Bitterness destroys us physically, destroys our capacity to love, and can infect those with whom we come in contact. We should allow God to use His largest spade and literally tear out that bitter root before it grows and we ourselves become useless as believers (Heb. 12:15).

Hostility is also destructive and contagious, but hostility is not born overnight. Lester Sumrall explains that hostility is born "out of the festering brew of unconfessed and unresolved hatred, anger, fear, and resentment." He adds that we should "carefully define hostility *not* as the flash of emotion that comes in response to a painful or unpleasant situation, but rather as the result of harboring those feelings in an unforgiving attitude of resentment" *(Hostility,* Thomas Nelson, p. 11).

Hatred is closely related to resentment, bitterness, and hostility. "Hate is a desire to hurt, to make another pay. Some common ways it expresses itself are: criticism, name-calling, snubbing, getting even" (Dale E. Galloway, *Rebuild Your Life,* Tyndale House, pp. 48-49). To hate someone, especially our enemies, often seems easier than trying to love. But it brings dire results, for we become enslaved to the persons we hate.

Hate seldom hurts the person it is directed toward, but it always hurts the person who harbors it. One lady told me about a friend of hers who had been struck and killed by a drunk driver. She said she had hated the driver so intensely she didn't think she could hate him enough. Then one day she attended a Bible study where the subject of forgiveness was discussed. The Holy Spirit convicted this woman of her hatred and she asked God to forgive her, and He did. For the first time in months, she sensed rest and freedom. She realized how much her mind had been controlled by the one she had so hated. She had been enslaved to him as she tried to think of ways to get even.

Malice, a close cousin of hatred and resentment, exists where there is usually "a deep-seated and often unreasonable dislike that takes pleasure in seeing others suffer" (Herbert G. Lockyer, *The Sins of Saints,* Loizeaux Brothers, p. 197). But Peter warns, "Rid yourselves of all malice and all deceit, hypocrisy, envy, and slander of every kind" (1 Peter 2:1).

Other Attitudes

Pride is at the root of much of our unforgiveness. Because pride can prevent us from forgiving, excessive pride is often a characteristic of the unforgiving person. That person believes, "I'm far more superior than the person who hurt me. I don't need him (or her), so I don't need to forgive."

Richard Anderson, author of *The Love Formula,* calls this type of pride, "a hard, cruel, and unforgiving taskmaster. It argues for a victory. It seeks to win over others, to dominate, to have the last word, to crush the opponent. It runs away from mercy, it forgets forgiveness, it ignores love" (Concordia Publishing, p. 45).

Jealousy and envy are two other attitudes often prominent in the unforgiving person. In her book *I Was a Battered Child,* Ruth Elizabeth Baird defines jealousy well; "Jealousy is feeling inferior and seeing or believing that someone has something you should have but don't" (Tyndale House, p. 96). Because Ruth was beaten and abused by her parents, she began to think she wasn't worth much. Feelings of jealousy arose when she saw the advantages of others.

But Ruth is not unique. We all feel inferior to some degree. We've all struggled with jealousy. When someone who we think is better off than we are hurts us, we often cannot forgive because of our jealousy.

If left unchecked, jealousy can turn into envy. "Envy, first cousin of jealousy, goes beyond that emotion to a kind of hatred. Envy says, 'Not only do I not like you being or having a certain something, I want it for myself at your expense'" (Jeanette Lockerbie, *Forgive, Forget and Be Free,* Christian Herald Books, p. 104). Like jealousy, envy can hinder or prevent forgiveness.

What are some of the other characteristics of the unforgiving person?

Guilt. As Christians, we owe forgiveness to those who offend us because of the forgiveness we have received from God (Eph. 4:32; Col. 3:13). God expects us and commands us to forgive. Yet when the Holy Spirit reminds us of our unforgiveness, we often feel guilty.

Anxiety, and its twin *worry,* attack us when we are uneasy over an anticipated danger or misfortune—some event we think will go badly for us. As they relate to forgiveness, anxiety and worry can strike while we are holding an unforgiving spirit because we may be expecting to be hurt again and again. When we are expecting to be hurt, we will lack confidence in the person or situation. This can lead to another fruit—*distrust.*

The person who refuses to forgive himself or others is unable to form close and lasting friendships. Because God has created all of us with the need for human love and companionship, loneliness is inevitable for the unforgiving person.

Woe Is Me!
Self-pity, that feeling that no one has been hurt as much as we have, can blind us. "There is no way we can understand or empathize with another person while we are locked in our pity"

(Creath Davis, *How to Win in a Crisis,* Zondervan, p. 47). When we can't understand why someone did something to us, we can have problems forgiving.

Tim LaHaye notes that self-pity is a denial of the biblical principle found in Romans 8:28: "And we know that in all things God works for the good of those who love Him, who have been called according to His purpose." This does not guarantee that all things that happen to us will be good or enjoyable, but the net result of all things will be good. God uses all things to conform us to His Son's image. We often overlook the truth found in the next verse. "For those God foreknew He also predestined to be conformed to the likeness of His Son, that he might be the firstborn among many brothers" (v. 29; see also Gal. 4:19). Meditating on Romans 8:28 *and* 29 and accepting it will remove our excuse for self-pity and free us to forgive.

Body Signals

In a highly publicized *Ladies' Home Journal* article, Anita Bryant discussed her stormy 20-year marriage and subsequent divorce from her husband Bob Green. Anita said her husband had used, abused, and rejected her for years. What were the results? Anita suffered from severe tension headaches, chest pains, arthritic flare-ups, and muscle spasms. A doctor told Anita her physical symptoms were the result of anger, frustration, and years of no communication (Cliff Jahr, "Anita Bryant's Startling Reversal," *Ladies Home Journal,* December 1980, p. 66).

Research has shown that the negative emotions that often accompany unforgiveness, particularly when those emotions are repressed, can cause or aggravate disease. Dr. S.I. McMillen in his book *None of These Diseases,* explains how our emotions produce changes in our body. "The emotional center produces these widespread changes by means of three principal mechanisms: by changing the amount of blood flowing to an organ; by affecting the secretions of certain glands; and by changing the tension of muscles" (Revell, p. 59).

Dr. McMillen goes on to document how emotional stress can cause or aggravate a host of disorders including ulcers, constipation, diarrhea, high blood pressure, headaches, diabetes, asthma, hives, hay fever, backaches, muscle spasms, arthritis, infections, heart attacks, colitis, high cholesterol, and exhaustion.

Though the results are inconclusive, some researchers have even suggested that negative emotions are a factor in developing cancer. Other researchers suggest that a happy person is a healthier person. The happy person does not get sick as often, recovers quicker when he is sick, and tends to live longer. Statistics have shown there are more heart attacks on Mondays than there are on Fridays when people are looking forward to the weekend.

Though there are many causes of depression, refusing to forgive can play a prominent role in this condition. Called America's number one emotional disorder, symptoms include an inability to enjoy anything, indecision, lack of concentration, no energy, tiredness, irritability, sleeplessness—a general lack of feeling (Bill Stearns, *From Rock Bottom to Mountaintop,* Victor Books, pp. 131-132).

"Depression tackles you when you . . . decide *not* to feel. . . . If you want to stay away from depression . . . acknowledge feelings you have" (Stearns, *From Rock Bottom,* pp. 134-135).

Forgiveness plays an important role in curing depression. Tim LaHaye explains, "Depressed-prone individuals are always conscious of a loved one or relative who rejected or injured them earlier in life. Until they forgive that person, they will never know lasting victory over depression" *(How to Win over Depression,* p. 198).

LaHaye also advises the unforgiving person to go to the person he resents, *if* the other person is aware of the resentment, and ask that person for forgiveness. Clearly, forgiveness can be an important weapon in defeating depression.

The Action Fruits

In addition to certain emotions, depression, and disease, unforgiveness can be at the root of some of our actions. When faced with serious personal problems, some people will turn to alcohol or drugs to deaden their emotional pain. Some turn to food, gambling, infidelity, or excessive work.

Other people become chronic complainers. But a Christian who complains is denying some basic principles of Scripture: "Godliness with contentment is great gain" (1 Tim. 6:6); "Be content with what you have" (Heb. 13:5); "Always giving thanks to God the Father for everything, in the name of our Lord Jesus Christ" (Eph. 5:20). "It is folly to complain if we accept that a God who loves us and cannot err is the one who orders our life" (Herbert G. Lockyer, *The Sins of Saints,* p. 96). Complaint can easily give way to gossip, sarcasm, slander, and arguments.

Cruelty, those deliberate acts designed to cause suffering, pain or distress, is yet another action fruit.

What About Divorce?

There are two different ways this fruit of unforgiveness can manifest itself: from an offense or several offenses committed within the marriage; or from an offense committed outside the relationship. It's possible for a single event to cause a marriage to break up. But more often divorce results when a series of offenses and problems accumulate unforgiven till the resulting resentment and bitterness crowd out love and commitment. Even events that occur outside the marriage relationship and go unforgiven can put a strain on the relationship and possibly result in divorce. Ben and Sandy's story is a good example. Forgiveness, both within and outside the marriage, is vital to keeping a marriage alive and growing.

Our Creativity Suffers

When we allow anger and unforgiveness to take over in our lives, our thinking becomes clouded. It becomes difficult to concentrate. As a result, our work and creativity become impaired. Jeanette Lockerbie, author of more than 20 books, confessed to this problem in *Forgive, Forget and Be Free*.

> Then one day it came to me that I was having a dearth of ideas for my writing. The creative juices were not flowing as formerly. Why? Bitterness, self-pity and resentment were clogging the stream of creativity (Christian Herald Books, p. 136).

Lockerbie plucked this fruit from her life and so should we if we truly desire to be creative sons and daughters of God.

The Violent Fruits

As 15 chained prisoners were being led from a paddy wagon to a courthouse, a man stepped from the onlooking crowd, pulled out a .38-caliber pistol and fired 6 shots into one of the prisoners. The prisoner had been accused of killing the man's 2 sons and was on his way to trial. The father had chosen the way of revenge rather than forgiveness.

Revenge, according to the dictionary, is inflicting punishment or injury in return for a wrong done. The word revenge often conjures up images of murder and violence, and there's no doubt that is revenge. But there are also more subtle modes of revenge: giving someone a cold shoulder, not talking to someone, or assassinating a person's character. Revenge—in any form—is forbidden by God (Rom. 12:17-21).

Suicide can even be a fruit of unforgiveness, particularly when someone has problems forgiving himself.

> To what extent do unforgiving attitudes enter into suicide? It is known that when unresolved conflicts and anxieties become unbearable, self-destruction seems more desirable for the depressed individual than trying to cope with the problems of life. Stormy personal relationships, broken romances, inability to make or keep friends—these are all determining causes in suicide (Helen Hosier, *It Feels Good to Forgive,* Harvest House, p. 33).

Other factors in suicide include guilt, feelings of worthlessness, depression, hostility, and anger at self and others.

Examples from Scripture

The Bible gives some clear examples of what happens when people live with the fruit of unforgiveness. The story of Cain's jealously of his brother Abel is found in the Book of Genesis. Abel had presented the Lord with a favorable sacrifice, but Cain's sacrifice was not acceptable. The Lord asked Cain why he was angry. "Why is your face downcast? If you do what is right, will you not be accepted? But if you do not do what is right, sin is crouching at your door; it desires to have you, but you must master it" (Gen. 4:6-7).

Later Cain asked his brother to go into the field with him. There Cain attacked Abel and killed him. The fruit of unforgiveness resulted in the first murder on Planet Earth.

Second Samuel 13 gives the account of the rape of Tamar by her half-brother Amnon. Tamar's brother Absalom hated Amnon for committing such an act. For two years he plotted revenge and finally had Amnon murdered for what he had done. But this fruit of unforgiveness had bitter consequences. The murder disrupted Absalom's relationship with his father King David. Because David was unable to offer true forgiveness to Absalom, Absalom began to plot against his father. After several years Absalom was killed in an armed rebellion he led against King David (2 Sam. 18).

Taking Inventory

How can we tell if we have an unforgiving spirit? By the fruit in our lives. Check yourself with these questions:

- Am I angry, resentful, bitter, and hostile?
- Is there someone I hate?
- Is my pride, jealousy, or envy telling me there is someone I need to cut from my life?
- Am I anxious or distrustful?
- Do I pity myself?

- Are there people I constantly criticize?
- Am I lonely?
- Do I constantly dwell on my injuries?
- Do I plot revenge?
- Do I refuse to talk to certain people?
- Have my feelings been hurt?
- Do I feel like someone has let me down?

A yes answer to any of these questions could indicate that there is something you need to forgive. If you don't forgive, you cannot be like Christ.

Just before Leonardo da Vinci commenced work on his famous "Last Supper," he had a violent quarrel with a fellow painter. The enraged and bitter Leonardo determined to take revenge by painting the face of his enemy, the other artist, into the face of Judas. But when he came to paint the face of Christ, he could make no progress. Something held him back, frustrating his best efforts. He came to the conclusion that it was because he had painted his enemy into the face of Judas. He erased the face of Judas and commenced anew on the face of Jesus, a success acclaimed by the ages.

That is a profound parable of the Christian life. You cannot at one and the same time be painting the features of Christ into your own life, and painting another face with the colors of enmity and hatred (Ella May Miller, *A Woman in Her Home,* Moody Press, pp. 114-115).

Why Do We Need to Forgive?
"But it is so hard to forgive," many have said.

My dear 95-year-old mother, who is still growing in Christ, says, "No, it isn't hard to forgive. It is much harder to carry the tremendously heavy burden of unforgiveness, hate, and resentment. That can break us down completely. Forgiveness heals and frees."

Hatred and hostilities will go with us to our graves and God will not overrule if we are not willing to forgive. It is to our advantage to forgive. But it is also for the benefit of the offender that God asks us to extend forgiveness. Our forgiveness of our fellow men and women is an example of the forgiveness God extends to us through Christ.

6
Who Do We Forgive? How Often?

If your brother sins against you seven times in a day, and seven times comes back to you and says, "I repent," forgive him (Luke 17:4).

A woman approached me one morning after a meeting and vehemently announced, "I'm so angry at God for giving my brother-in-law a heart attack and killing him!"

People often become angry at God and feel honest hatred for Him because affliction and devastation has hit them or their loved ones. This woman had become so angry, in a sense, she needed to forgive God for treating her and her sister so "unfairly" if she ever expected to realize freedom in her life. Of course, God never makes an error. He has never done anything to warrant our forgiveness. But if we believe He has failed us, we cannot grow spiritually.

We, as Christians, often forget we are in the ebb and flow of life here on Planet Earth, a world in which sin and Satan rule. The rain falls on the righteous and the unrighteous (Matt. 5:45). If we accept God's sunshine and warmth, we must also accept the thunder and lightning. If I am in the pathway of a tornado, I will suffer loss as well as my neighbors. Yes, God "allows it," but He doesn't purposely and directly "plan" it that way. He *could* intervene because He is God, and often He does, but many times He does not. We will not understand the thousand "whys" till we stand face to face with Christ.

I know God was not shocked at this woman's anger, because He is unshockable. God has shown me that I too am capable of anger toward Him. I find He continually uncovers heart attitudes I didn't even realize existed. Just because God has miraculously placed forgiveness in my heart for a criminal doesn't mean I have spiritually "arrived."

My late brother, a member of God's family and a minister of the Gospel, had a kidney transplant after being ill for more than a dozen years. For some time he had been on a kidney machine three times weekly for dialysis. At 3 A.M. one morning he received a telephone call from his surgeon saying he was to come into the hospital immediately. They had a kidney for him.

There had been much prayer for my brother from his family and his many friends who loved him. We were all notified. We were exuberant, and oh, how we prayed the transplant would be successful. We felt no one deserved this more.

I'm told there is a 50 percent chance a person's body will accept a new organ after a transplant. That morning four transplants took place. Two were accepted by the recipients and two were rejected. My brother's was rejected.

At first he felt wonderful. He said he believed he knew how Lazarus must have felt when Jesus called him forth from the grave. He was feeling like a new man with brand new life. We praised the Lord for His goodness.

Approximately three weeks later, we received word that his new kidney was to be removed; his body would not accept it. The kidney had become enlarged and infected and my brother was very ill.

I truly felt frustration and anger . . . at who? It had to be at God. It wasn't my brother's fault, nor the surgeon's. Certainly those of us who had prayed so fervently couldn't be blamed. I was *angry* at God! I actually shook my fist in the air and asked, "Why?" I hadn't even asked *why* when Diane died. I could accept that as an answer to the prayer I had prayed prior to her death. But my brother?

"God," I demanded, "I haven't bothered You very often regarding the physical health of my loved ones. I have prayed often for others, but I haven't asked much for my own family. Now here is my brother, Your child, who needed Your touch and a healthy kidney. What is wrong with our family that You won't meet our physical needs for health and strength? How come so many others get Your attention and we don't?"

I began to weep as I recognized my anger. "Oh, God, forgive me. How could I become angry at You? I am so sorry. My brother is still Your child. You love him more than his wife or his children or I do. He is in Your hands. . . . Forgive me Father for becoming angry with You. Cleanse me through Christ's blood. Fill me with love and complete confidence in You. Amen."

My brother went back on dialysis for about a year before he was offered another opportunity for a transplant. The doctor warned him there were dangers involved, but my brother decided to go ahead with the operation anyway. When my sister-in-law told me about the transplant, I prayed that the operation would be successful. But I also promised God that no matter what the outcome, I would not get angry.

Three weeks after the transplant my brother died due to complications. But this time, not once was I tempted to get angry at God. I could only look at his death with a sense of joy. My brother is with Christ now. He will no longer be sick or in pain. I don't understand why God allowed his death, but I was able to accept it as God's way of dealing with the situation.

These two stories illustrate several of the reasons why we get angry with God: circumstances over which we have no control, unmet expectations, disappointments, unanswered prayers, and suffering. Behind each of these reasons for our anger lies a basic spiritual problem—unbelief.

Think about it a moment. Either God is in control of this universe or He isn't. Either God is correct in His dealings with us or He's mistaken. Either God does what He promises or He doesn't. Our anger toward God, no matter how justified we may feel, indicates we don't believe God is in control. We don't believe He's correct or fair or that He keeps His promises.

Of all the people we need to forgive, God should be first on our lists. Without a healthy relationship with God, we cannot be at peace with ourselves or others. We cannot truly forgive and love ourselves or others when we're holding a grudge against God.

Our unbelief often stems from our misconceptions of the character of God. Some of us view Him as an angry, mean, "I'm-gonna-get-you" kind of God, who sits in heaven waiting to destroy us as soon as we make one wrong move. Others view Him as disinterested, uncaring, unloving. Still others view Him as the over indulging grandfather type who spoils His children, letting them do whatever they please.

How does an adult wind up with an inadequate and limiting concept of God? Usually, it's because we have entered adulthood with ideas about God that seemed to serve us well in childhood. The problem is that childish ideas about God and spiritual growth just don't go together. Those who study the child's concept of God tell me that because of the undeveloped state of the child's intellect, he must view God in very concrete terms. The idea of the spiritual nature of the Father may be difficult for some adults—but it is impossible for children. Somehow, the child's God is always a big, strong person—a bigger, stronger version of his earthly father. After all, he is taught to call God 'Father'; so the association between the father he sees and knows and the One he cannot see is formed (Donald L. Anderson, *Better Than Blessed,* Tyndale House, p. 64).

What Is God Really Like?

One common view of God is that He is all love and would never allow unhappiness to touch His children. But people who believe this are often confused when they see suffering in the world or experience despair and tragedy in their own lives.

At the opposite extreme is the view that God is a stern judge just waiting to pronounce sentence on wrongdoing. The people who see God in this manner are often afraid of Him and afraid of making one wrong move. Fear prevents them from enjoying their relationship with God. But both viewpoints are wrong.

God is love *and* God is just, *but* He is so much more. To know God as He really is, we must study the Word. The Bible shows us many facets of God's character. Let's look at a few of them.

God is *emotional.* He experiences sorrow (Gen. 6:6); anger (Ex. 22:22-24; Num. 25:4); jealousy (Ex. 20:5; Deut. 32:16); joy (Zeph. 3:17; Prov. 11:20); and love and compassion (Deut. 30:3; 2 Kings 13:23; Ex. 33:19; John 3:16; Hosea 3:1).

God is *eternal.* He has always existed and will never cease to exist. "The Lord will reign for ever and ever" (Ex. 15:18; see also Job 36:26; Ps. 9:7; Lam. 5:19; Rev. 1:8).

God is *faithful.* The psalmist declares, "Your love, O Lord, reaches to the heavens, your faithfulness to the skies" (Ps. 36:5; see also Ps. 89:1; 1 Cor. 1:9; 1 John 1:9).

God is *forgiving.* "The Lord our God is merciful and forgiving, even though we have rebelled against Him" (Dan. 9:9; see also Ps. 32:1).

God is *good.* "Praise the Lord, for the Lord is good" (Ps. 135:3; see also Matt. 19:17; Pss. 25:8; 118:1).

God is *holy.* "The Lord said to Moses, 'Speak to the entire assembly of Israel and say to them: Be holy because I, the Lord your God, am holy'" (Lev. 19:1-2; see also Heb. 12:10).

God is *just;* He is always fair to Himself and man. "He is the Rock, His works are perfect, and all His ways are just. A faithful God who does no wrong, upright and just is He" (Deut. 32:4; see also Ps. 103:6).

God is *kind*. "But love your enemies, do good to them, and lend to them without expecting to get anything back. Then your reward will be great, and you will be sons of the Most High, because He is kind to the ungrateful and wicked" (Luke 6:35; see also Jer. 31:3).

God is *love*. "Whoever does not love does not know God, because God is love" (1 John 4:8; see also John 3:16).

God is *merciful*. "Be merciful, just as your Father is merciful" (Luke 6:36; see also Jer. 3:12).

God *never changes;* He's always consistent. "God is not a man, that He should lie, nor a son of man, that He should change His mind. Does He speak and then not act? Does He promise and not fulfill?" (Num. 23:19; see also Mal. 3:6).

God is *omnipotent* or all-powerful. "For nothing is impossible with God" (Luke 1:37; see also Job 42:1-2; Matt. 19:26; Mark 14:36).

God is *omnipresent* or everywhere at once. "Where can I go from Your Spirit? Where can I flee from Your presence? If I go up to the heavens, You are there; if I make my bed in the depths, You are there" (Ps. 139:7-8; see also Acts 17:27).

God is *omniscient* or all-knowing. Nothing ever takes Him by surprise. "God . . . knows everything" (1 John 3:20; see also Ps. 147:5; Prov. 15:3; Heb. 4:13).

God is *righteous*. Everything He does is right and perfect. He can do no wrong. "The Lord is righteous in all His ways and loving toward all He has made" (Ps. 145:17; see also Ps. 119:137; 1 John 2:29).

God is *sovereign,* or in other words, He is the supreme ruler over all the earth. He answers to no one, for there is no one higher or greater than He. "Acknowledge and take to heart this day that the Lord is God in heaven above and on the earth below. There is no other" (Deut. 4:39; see also Pss. 47:2; 83:18; Dan. 4:35; Acts 17:24; Isa. 45:21; NIV 1 Chron. 29:11).

"God is *spirit,* and His worshipers must worship in spirit and in truth" (John 4:24; see also Gen. 1:2).

God is absolute *truth* and reality. "For the Word of the Lord is right and true; He is faithful in all He does (Ps. 33:4; see also 1 Kings 18:24).

God knows how to express one characteristic without compromising another, such as expressing His love without negating His justice. That's what He did when He sent Jesus Christ to the cross to die for our sins.

But what is God really like? Our best example is Jesus Christ. Jesus said, "I and the Father are One" (John 10:30).

> Jesus showed us God as He is and wants to be known. While the total being of God is more than could be revealed in Jesus, this is the best image that a person can gain of the true nature of the heavenly Father. Being sensitive to what God shows and tells us about Himself in Jesus Christ inevitably brings about a shift in our God-concept. It gets us ready to make mature responses to God (Donald L. Anderson, *Better Than Blessed,* p. 66).

It's very possible if we have a wrong or childish concept of God, we could be angry at a god who does not exist.

Sources of Anger

Let's look at four broad categories where we can place most of the anger directed toward God: circumstances, unmet expectations and the resultant disappointments, unanswered prayer, and suffering.

Whenever we complain about the circumstances (every day details) of life, in reality, we are complaining about the way God is ordering our lives. Our complaining reveals our doubts that God is really sovereign, just, kind, righteous, all-knowing, and always acting out of love.

Misconceptions about God and Christianity abound today. One is that once we become Christians, we will no longer have any problems. That is simply not true. The Bible often refers to the trials and problems of this life. But no matter what the circumstances, we have the promise that Jesus will help us face our problems.

Related to the first area is a second reason we often get angry with God: when our expectations aren't met. We expect God to do some favor or some miracle for us and when He doesn't, we conclude He isn't God—or if He is, He isn't interested in us. It could be that our expectations are unmet because we have unrealistic expectations based on a false concept of God. Or perhaps God is simply trying to teach us to trust Him and Him only. Erwin Lutzer has an interesting insight on this. He asks, "Have you ever thought of the fact that our disappointments are God's way of reminding us that there are idols in our lives that must be dealt with?" The challenge of disappointment, he concludes, is to continue to be obedient *(Managing Your Emotions,* Christian Herald Books, pp. 122, 126).

Many times we become angry when it seems God doesn't answer prayer. There could be many reasons for unanswered prayer. There may be unforgiveness or other sins in our lives. Or perhaps the prayer wasn't offered in faith (Heb. 11:6; James 1:6) or the matter for which we are praying is not in God's will (1 John 5:14-15). Craig Massey offers another explanation for unanswered prayer in his book *Adjust or Self-Destruct.*

> It may come as a surprise, but it is true: the believer's old nature delights in praying just as much as his new nature delights in praying. The similarity stops there, however, because the old nature, while praying vigorously, prays in an entirely different way than the new nature. The old nature cries out for worldly benefits, comfort, personal fulfillment, physical well-being, emotional tranquility, and mental achievement. . . . The old nature's prayer life is egocentric and selfish. In essence, the old nature demands, "I want what I want, God! I want it when I want it, and I want it right now!" (Moody Press, p. 98)

When we are not praying properly, can we really be angry with God when there are no results?

From brief periods of emotional or physical pain to intense

lingering agony, suffering is part of most of our lives. When we are suffering it is easy to point an angry finger at God and demand, "Why? Why me?" Scores of books have been written and numerous sermons have been preached on the why of suffering. But there's not always a clear-cut answer—and that's the hardest spiritual fact of life to grasp.

Don't Try to Hide It

Though we may try, it is impossible to hide our anger at God from God. Not only is it impossible, it's unnecessary. God allows us to be angry at Him. Moses expressed his anger and frustration when the Children of Israel were complaining about their diet of manna (Num. 11:11-15). Did God zap Moses for his outburst? No. He devised a way to help Moses "carry the burden of the people" (vv. 16-17).

The Prophet Jonah became angry at God when He spared the wicked people of Nineveh from destruction (Jonah 4). Did God punish Jonah for expressing his anger? No. "We may have expected the Lord to dispatch a quick lightning bolt to remove all signs of Jonah. A great voice would say, 'There now, Jonah. Just what you deserve for being angry with Me.'" But God tenderly transformed Jonah's emotions to help him feel what the Lord felt about those lost people of Nineveh" (Barry Applewhite, *Feeling Good About Your Feelings,* Victor Books, p. 41).

The Prophet Habakkuk also cried out in anger to God. Habakkuk was angry at God for His silence over the wickedness of the Children of Israel. Did God destroy Habakkuk for his anger? No. God revealed to the prophet His plan for punishing Israel (Hab. 1:2-11).

Because these Old Testament men became angry at God doesn't mean that anger at God is appropriate. God's righteousness prevents Him from doing any wrong, and so it is never right for anyone to be angry at God. But God loves us and understands us as we are. We don't have to pretend with Him. Only as we are honest with Him and, like Moses, Jonah, and Habakkuk, admit our anger can He help us deal with it.

Resolving Our Anger Toward God

Unlike God, our viewpoint of life is very limited. We cannot see within people's hearts, nor can we predict their reactions or see into the future. Because of this, it may be days, weeks, or even years before we understand why God allowed a certain thing to happen. Sometimes we may never understand, but that is the essence of faith: trusting God when we don't understand.

Resolving our anger toward God—forgiving Him—is actually a matter of repenting or changing our attitude toward God. First we need to admit our anger. Remember, God is not shocked by our admission; He is aware of the anger even before we are. Second, we need to tell God why we are angry. We should be specific. We need to ask forgiveness for our unbelief and then repent: change our attitude toward Him, our hearts, and our minds. As we get to know God better through reading His Word, it will become easier to change our attitude toward Him.

And last, let's ask God to help us cultivate an attitude of acceptance. Being able to accept whatever comes our way will help us to "forgive" God when we are tempted to be angry with Him.

Forgive God for Yourself

Many people cannot accept the way God made them. They think they are either too short or too tall. Or perhaps they think their hair is the wrong color. Or their eyes. Or they are not quite as bright as they'd like to be. Rejection of our appearance, intelligence, and abilities is rejection of God's wisdom and control. It's evidence that we really don't believe God is sovereign.

But God was at work designing us even while we were in our mother's womb. "For You created my inmost being; You knit me together in my mother's womb. I praise You because I am fearfully and wonderfully made; Your works are wonderful, I know that full well. My frame was not hidden from You when I was made in the secret place. When I was woven together in the depths of the earth, Your eyes saw my unformed body. All the days ordained for me were written in Your Book before one of them came to be" (Ps. 139:13-16).

God takes responsibility for our handicaps. "The Lord said to him, 'Who gave man his mouth? Who makes him deaf or dumb? Who gives him sight or makes him blind? Is it not I, the Lord?'" (Ex. 4:11)

And Paul tells us God is responsible for our abilities. "For who makes you different from anyone else? What do you have that you did not receive? And if you did receive it, why do you boast as though you did not?" (1 Cor. 4:7)

God made us with our respective faults and assets for a special reason. Until we accept ourselves—faults and all—we will have difficulty trusting God's wisdom in other areas of our lives. Because we tend to transfer to others the attitude we have about ourselves, if we do not accept ourselves, we will also have difficulty accepting others (Charles L. Allen, *The Secret of Abundant Living,* Revell, p. 17). All of our relationships are affected by our lack of self-acceptance.

We can learn to accept ourselves by admitting to God we cannot accept ourselves, asking forgiveness for our wrong attitudes, and then thanking God for making us the way He did. We should meditate on Psalm 139 and on other passages that describe God's sovereignty. We shouldn't get discouraged if we don't automatically feel good about ourselves. Sometimes it takes awhile to learn this lesson.

Why We Can't Forgive Ourselves

Joyce (not her real name) is 38, divorced, and the mother of 3. "There are things I can't forgive myself for doing," she said, referring to her decision to leave a troubled marriage. "Some of my decisions adversely affected others and I see the results every day."

Joyce is like many of us. Even if we can forgive God for who we are, we may still be unable to forgive ourselves for what we've done or have neglected to do. Much of our anger within ourselves stems from our misconceptions about God's forgiveness of us.

Many people have no problem believing they are saved by faith, but they think they can only keep their salvation by following all of God's rules and doing good works. But this is a gross perversion of the Gospel.

> God has never, and will never, deal with us only on the basis of our goodness or successes. Our relationship to Him began with His forgiveness and continues because He continues to forgive us. . . . Many persons who admit that their life in Christ began when they accepted His free forgiveness now seem to feel that they must rely on their own goodness—or their own great strides of spiritual growth—to keep the Father happy with them. Not so. Our relationship with God has its beginning in His grace and continues to rest on that foundation (Donald L. Anderson, *Better Than Blessed,* pp. 35-36).

We are not perfect—just forgiven. We will continue to sin and to make mistakes. All of us struggle with failure. The Apostle Paul did (Rom. 7:7-25). Yet he is considered to be a spiritual giant.

If we have received Christ, all of our sins—past, present, and future—have already been forgiven. We cannot take Christ by surprise. We can do nothing that He has not already forgiven. When we don't see ourselves as forgiven or measuring up before God, we are looking at *our* actions rather than at Christ and what He did for us on the cross (Peter E. Gilquist, *Love Is Now,* Zondervan, p. 23).

"As far as the east is from the west, so far has He removed our transgressions from us" (Ps. 103:12). Notice the psalmist didn't say as far as the north is from the south. That's a distance that can be measured. The distance between east and west cannot be measured; it's a poetic way of describing infinity (Judson Cornwall, *Let Us Enjoy Forgiveness,* Revell, p. 149).

"When you were dead in your sins and in the uncircumcision

of your sinful nature, God made you alive with Christ. He forgave us all our sins" (Col. 2:13). Paul didn't say we were only forgiven for some sins or only for the ones committed prior to the time we accepted Christ. "He forgave us all our sins." That means past, present, and future—the big ones and the little ones—the ones that hurt others and the ones that only hurt ourselves. "Therefore, there is now no condemnation for those who are in Christ Jesus" (Rom. 8:1).* Forgiveness is a fact.

"By one sacrifice He has made perfect forever those who are being made holy" (Heb. 10:14). Which sacrifice is the writer talking about? Christ's death on the cross. Who is perfect forever? Anyone who receives Christ.

A Christian who refuses to forgive himself insults God and, in a sense, is elevating himself above God.

> If God has forgiven us all our sins . . . what should our attitude be about sin in ourselves and others? For me to fail to forgive myself or anyone else who has offended me is to say that I have a higher standard of forgiveness than God, because whatever it is that has so hurt me that I can't forgive it, God already has (Hal Lindsey, *The Liberation of Planet Earth,* Zondervan, pp. 170, 172).

Christians who have difficulty forgiving themselves can learn from the Apostle Paul's attitude. Paul had persecuted and hunted down members of the early church. He had every reason to refuse to forgive himself and live a life of regret. But did he? Instead he said, "For I am the least of the apostles and do not even deserve to be called an apostle, because I persecuted the church of God. But by the grace of God I am what I am, and His grace to me was not without effect. No, I worked harder than all of them—yet not I, but the grace of God that was with me" (1 Cor. 15:9-10).

By recognizing and accepting the completeness of God's

---

*Sin does affect our relationship with God, but not our legal standing with Him. Please see chapter 11, "The Other Side of Forgiveness."

forgiveness, Paul could accept and forgive himself. He focused on the future instead of regretting the past. "Not that I have already obtained all this, or have already been made perfect, but I press on to take hold of that for which Christ Jesus took hold of me. . . . Forgetting what is behind and straining toward what is ahead, I press on toward the goal to win the prize for which God has called me heavenward in Christ Jesus" (Phil. 3:12-14).

But I Can't Be Forgiven!"

For one reason or another, many people think they are beyond God's forgiveness. Sometimes this feeling comes because people tend to rank sins, placing some in the "easy to forgive" category, some in the "hard to forgive" category, and the rest in the "unforgivable" category. In some churches, divorce is the unforgivable sin. In others it's abortion or murder or homosexuality. But in God's eyes, there is no ranking of sins. He is no respecter of persons. (See 1 Peter 1:17.)

When a woman who had been caught in the very act of adultery was brought before Jesus, He forgave her (John 8:1-11). The saints in the church at Corinth had among their members former idolaters, male prostitutes, homosexuals, thieves, and drunkards (1 Cor. 6:9-11).

There is one sin, however, that God cannot forgive. Jesus explained, "And so I tell you, every sin and blasphemy will be forgiven men, but the blasphemy against the Spirit will not be forgiven. Anyone who speaks a word against the Son of Man will be forgiven, but anyone who speaks against the Holy Spirit will not be forgiven, either in this age or in the age to come" (Matt. 12:31-32).

What was Jesus talking about? After Jesus healed a demon-possessed man, the Pharisees had accused Him of casting out demons through Satanic power. These religious leaders were so spiritually blind and morally bankrupt, they didn't recognize Jesus, nor were they interested in accepting His forgiveness. Jesus told them their rejection of Him was unforgivable.

Today, many commentators agree, the only unforgivable sin is to refuse to accept God's forgiveness through Jesus Christ. God cannot forgive us when we reject Christ, our one and only provision for forgiveness.

If you're afraid of being guilty of the unforgivable sin, take heart. Your concern is evidence you're not beyond forgiveness. Reach out and take the pardon God offers through Jesus Christ.

Forgiving Others

Once we are at peace with God and ourselves, it is time to forgive others. Who are these others we may need to forgive? Anyone who offends, hurts, abuses, or angers us. I will list as many of these others as I can think of to help us search our own memories. Let's take a moment to ask God to reveal to us the people in our lives we may need to forgive. Perhaps it will help to have paper and pencil ready to jot down our own list of others.

1. God made us exactly as we are for His own special purpose. Two tools He uses to mold us are our *parents.* Realizing this can free us to forgive our parents for their shortcomings and mistakes.

2. The relationship between a Christian *husband and wife* should illustrate the relationship between Jesus Christ and His church. Love and forgiveness characterize the relationship between Christ and His church. Therefore, love and forgiveness should be an integral part of Christian marriage.

3. It's important for those who are divorced to forgive their former *spouses.* It will promote emotional and spiritual healing in the life of the divorced person and his or her children.

4. Because a child's concept of God is so much influenced by the child's relationship with his parents, parents should be models of God's unconditional love and forgiveness to their *children.*

5. We must forgive *other family members,* including broth-

ers and sisters, aunts and uncles, grandparents, cousins, and other relatives.

6. To keep unity in the body of Christ, we need to forgive our *fellow believers.* This includes our ministers or former ministers, deacons, Sunday School teachers, choir directors, youth workers—any leader or layman in our churches.

7. We must forgive *people from our past, including people who have died.* "Many people suppose that just because something happened 20 to 40 years ago, the emotions associated with it lie in the past, too," explains Dr. Cecil G. Osborne, director of the Burlingame Counseling Center in California. "However, we now know, and can demonstrate beyond all possibility of doubt, that even though the event is in the past, the feelings surrounding that event are still in us. If those emotions are unexpressed anger, fear, and hurt, they are doing great damage to us in the present" *(The Art of Getting Along with People,* Zondervan, p. 60).

8. We need to forgive *the person who attempts or commits suicide,* for our own healing and for the healing of the suicide victim's close friends and family members. Children, in particular, are terribly confused when a parent commits suicide. "Attitudes toward the deceased parent are extremely important. If the survivors show hostility toward the victim, the children will think they should (William L. Coleman, *Understanding Suicide,* David C. Cook Publishing, p. 147).

9. We need to forgive *those in authority,* remembering that no authority exists without the permission of God (Rom. 13:1). This includes government officials, police officers, and employers.

10. Forgive *our co-workers and business associates.*

11. Forgive *the people who have hurt our loved ones.*

12. Forgive *the person who commits a crime against us.*

13. Forgive *the trespassers in our lives,* those who may not have hurt us willfully.

14. Forgive *the persecutor,* the person who actively intimidates, assaults, attacks, or harasses us.

15. Forgive *our enemies,* the people who hate us.

How Many Times?

One day Jesus was teaching His disciples how to resolve a conflict with a Christian brother. "Lord, how many times shall I forgive my brother when he sins against me? Up to seven times?" Peter asked.

Peter, you see, thought he was quite generous because the rabbis of that day taught it was only necessary to forgive another three times (Warren W. Wiersbe, *Meet Yourself in the Parables,* Victor Books, p. 127).

But Jesus said, "No, Peter, not seven times, but seventy times seven." (See Matt. 18:21-22.)

Peter must have been shocked because Jesus was saying we should forgive always. Our ability to forgive is always an illustration to the world of God's forgiveness of us.

7

What Do We Forgive? When?

While they were stoning him, Stephen prayed, "Lord Jesus, receive my spirit." Then he fell on his knees and cried out, "Lord, do not hold this sin against them." When he had said this, he fell asleep (Acts 7:59-60).

By the time Margaret was 8 she was responsible for taking care of her 4 younger brothers and sisters. Her parents were alcoholics, frequently fought and, for the most part, ignored their 11 children.

Margaret remembers always being hungry, always having a gnawing stomach and headache. When there wasn't enough food in the house for all her younger brothers and sisters, which was often, Margaret went down to the local grocery where she stole fruit or donuts.

Whenever her dad beat her mother, Margaret tried to get between them to stop the fighting. On one occasion, she saw her dad rip her mother's clothes off. This confused her and she found herself hating her father.

When Margaret was 10, the state took her and her younger brothers and sisters away from her parents. For the next 18 months, Margaret was shuffled from one foster home to another—6 in all. Finally, a fine Christian couple took Margaret in and treated her as their own. A few months later, Margaret received Christ when an altar call was given at their church.

On Christmas Eve, when Margaret was 16, her dad unexpectedly came to the home of her foster parents. "I was deathly afraid of him," Margaret remembers. "I hated the ground he walked on. I didn't understand everything, but I just knew he'd never been a daddy to me."

Margaret tried to be polite. She knew that as a Christian, she had to love her dad. But when he laid $80 in her lap as a Christmas present, she jumped up, threw the money in his face and shouted, "You can never buy me back!"

She ran to her room upstairs. Her foster mother followed and gently said, "Margaret, you're a missionary to your family and you cannot act like this and be a Christian. I'm not saying it isn't hard. My heart bleeds for you. But you've got to go down and apologize to your father. He *is* your father."

Margaret knew this was right. She went back downstairs and said, "I'm sorry. I was wrong."

"Margaret, I'm a Christian now too," her dad said. "I heard of this good home you were in and I just had to come see you."

Margaret looks back on that meeting as the night she forgave her father. "After that when he'd come to visit, I'd be glad to see him," she says.

*   *   *

A young man named Stephen was brought before the Sanhedrin, a Jewish legislative body. Because false witnesses had accused him of blasphemy, an angry crowd dragged Stephen out of the city to stone him. And Stephen, the first Christian martyr, cried out, "Lord, do not hold this sin against them!" (See Acts 6:8—7:60.)

*   *   *

During the Korean war, a young Communist officer ordered the execution of a Christian civilian. When the officer learned the man ran an orphanage for small children, he decided to spare the man. Instead, he had the man's 19-year-old son shot.

Later, this same officer was tried and condemned to death for war crimes. But the Christian father intervened.

He said even though justice called for the man's execution, he felt the young, idealistic man had probably thought he was acting properly. "Give him to me," the father said, "and I'll teach him about the Saviour."

The father was allowed to take the young man into his home. There the young man learned about Christ and His forgiveness and later became a Christian pastor.

*   *   *

The young prophet's wife ran away from her husband and became one of the temple prostitutes. One day, when she was no longer useful at the temple, she was put on sale in the marketplace. Anyone with the right amount of money could have purchased and used her for any purpose, but her husband bought her and took her back home. (See Hosea 1—3.)

*   *   *

Could God really expect Margaret to forgive her father's neglect? Did He expect Stephen to forgive his murderers, or the Korean man his son's murderers? What about Hosea? Would God expect him to forgive his wife's infidelity?

The answer to every one of these questions is yes. In each of these situations, God expected these people to forgive and they did forgive. What does God expect us to forgive?

Forgive *That?*

We all have a tendency to rank sins. But when God commands us to forgive, He doesn't say, "Forgive everything but. . . ." He says, "Forgive." Whenever we decide something is unforgivable, we are taking God's place by being a judge (James 4:11-12). God's forgiveness flows freely to all types of people with all manner of sin. As His children can we dare do any less?

Often, after I have presented my testimony, someone will most surely say, "Yes, I agree, we as believers must be forgiving people, but certainly we aren't commanded or expected to forgive a heinous crime like that!"

Many Christians have adopted society's view that crime shouldn't be forgiven. The man in prison, particularly a rapist-murderer, is not thought of as a valuable human being. We are more than ready and willing to toss criminals out on a human garbage pile to decompose, to be completely forgotten. But God does not agree with this attitude. "The Lord . . . is patient with you, not wanting anyone to perish, but everyone to come to repentance" (2 Peter 3:9).

Jesus Christ forgave His murderers, and He did so while hanging between two thieves who were condemned to die. One of them repented of his sins and Christ forgave him in the midst of His own intense suffering. He said, "I tell you the truth, today you will be with Me in paradise" (Luke 23:43).

Because I was awakened to the importance of forgiveness through a crime, I have become sensitive to society's attitude toward crime and criminals. But crime is not the only offense we must forgive.

God expects us to forgive petty disturbances as well as large injustices, little hurts as well as deep ones. He expects us to forgive slights, real or imagined insults, rejection, hatred, and abuse. Let's list some of these things we must forgive.

But first take a moment to pray. Get out the list you started in the last chapter. Ask God to help you see what you need to forgive, then jot down the what next to the who.

What Is An Offense?
An offense is anything that breaks or transgresses a law, rule, or code of ethics. The term also refers to anything that would

hurt us or make us feel resentful. Something can offend us without breaking some type of law or rule or accepted standard of conduct. So it's possible for us to be offended by an action that would not necessarily offend someone else. We should keep this in mind while we are trying to decide what we may need to forgive. If something angers us or bothers us, we should forgive it. We don't need to deny our hurt and anger because someone else thinks we shouldn't feel that way. Let's learn to be honest with ourselves, with others, and with God.

1. We need to forgive *single offenses.* These are one-time only events. They may have been premeditated; they may have occurred through sheer ignorance. But this type of offense is not likely to happen again.

2. We need to forgive *repeated offenses.* Repeated offenses are likely to occur anytime we have a close relationship with another person. Anyone who is married can probably think something offensive that his or her spouse does time and time again.

3. We need to forgive *non-relationship offenses.* The offenders in these cases are not friends or relatives. These would include crimes, acts of violence, accidents, and other mishaps.

4. We need to forgive *something that offends or we think should have offended our loved ones.* We are not usually directly involved in these incidents.

5. We need to forgive *debts.* This could be an actual past due loan of money, or tools, or some other possession. Or a debt can be something that we think someone owes us: for example, a birthday card or Christmas present, or perhaps a compliment or thank you.

6. We need to forgive *trespasses,* the times when someone uses our property without our permission. Our property can include not only our material possessions but also our time, our talents, our reputation, our rights, and our comfort.

7. We need to forgive *persecution.* In this country, not many of us have been beaten or tortured for our faith. But we should forgive people who make fun of us or laugh at our beliefs.

8. We need to forgive the *things that rip and tear at the very core of our being and assault our self-image.* This includes insults, criticism, and rejection.

9. We need to forgive some people for their *good qualities or successes.* This probably sounds a bit unusual, but it is possible to become resentful toward another person's good fortune or talents. Joyce Landorf relates a good example of this.

> I found I had to forgive Dick [her husband] for a lot of things, including his being so smart. His mathe- matical knowledge has enabled him to be a fine banker. His coolness and even temperament have been an outstanding asset in every position he's held, and his ability to work conscientiously has pro- moted him to the top position in every job. It seems strange to say you have to forgive someone for these "good" things, but I realized that I had been resentful of all these attributes *(His Stubborn Love,* Zondervan, p. 99).

Once Joyce forgave her husband for his good qualities, her attitudes turned around. The things that had once bothered her now made her proud of her husband.

10. We need to forgive *sins against us.* Some types of offenses already listed could be sin—not all are. But whenever someone sins against us, that is, breaks God's Word in a way that directly affects us—we must forgive.

Forgive When?

Ephesians 4:26 advises us to deal with our anger before sundown. That means within the same day we are offended we are to resolve our anger and forgive. "Anger that persists beyond sundown is uncontrolled, and it is uncontrolled anger that causes our problems. It ruptures relationships, it stifles spiritual growth, it gives place to the devil and it opens the door to sinning" (Erwin Lutzer, *Managing Your Emotions,* Chris- tian Herald Books, p. 106).

Letting our anger smolder past sundown puts distance

between us and the offender and helps us forget that our offender is a real flesh and blood person with needs just like ours. It is better to forgive right away, not tonight or tomorrow or next week. We must also keep in mind that life is uncertain. A more convenient time may never come.

Some of us are just learning about forgiveness and may have carried anger and grudges for months or years. Others of us may have fallen into the habit of denying our emotions. Someone may make us angry, but we repress it and tell ourselves the anger isn't there. In those cases when the offense is long in the past, it's impossible for us to deal with our anger in the same day. We've missed that opportunity. But there's nothing stopping us from forgiving now. No matter when the offense occurred, as soon as we are aware of anger and unforgiveness we need to deal with it.

We can think of the offense as a wound. If a wound is not cleaned and bandaged, it becomes infected. If an offense is not cleaned with forgiveness and bandaged with love, it too can become infected with bitterness, resentment, hostility—any of the fruit of unforgiveness. The longer we wait, the worse the "infection" gets. To be healthy, we must deal with the offense right away. We don't have to wait until the offender asks our forgiveness or until we feel like forgiving. We can forgive now.

Always forgiving everyone everything immediately—in short, total forgiveness—is a large order to fill. But with God's help we can do it.

8
How to Forgive

Bear with each other and forgive whatever grievances you may have against one another. Forgive as
the Lord forgave you. And over all these virtues put
on love, which binds them all together in perfect
unity (Col. 3:13-14).

A little boy really wanted an ice cream cone one day, so he
asked his babysitter for some money. When his mother was
home, she always gave him the correct change—two quarters
—for ice cream. But on this day, the babysitter gave him a $1
bill—more than enough to buy the ice cream, but he didn't
realize that.

"How will I get the ice cream?" he asked, not realizing that he
had more than enough money to pay for it.

When it comes to spiritual things, we are often like the little
boy. In one hand we clutch the means to forgive people, but we
still ask, "How can I be like You, Lord? How can I follow Your
commands? How can I be loving and forgiving to others?"

We Have the Resources
God has given us everything we need to lead a holy life (2 Peter
1:3). Our three resources are Jesus Christ, the Holy Spirit, and

the Bible. But we often don't recognize our resources and when we don't use them, we don't grow spiritually.

How do these resources help us?

Christ told us to abide in Him (John 15:1-7). "I am the vine; you are the branches. If a man remains in Me and I in him, he will bear much fruit; apart from Me you can do nothing" (v. 5).

Abiding in Christ means depending on Him for all our needs on a moment by moment basis. Our dependence on Him yesterday will not help us today. Abiding today will not help us next month. Abiding must become a habit, a moment by moment awareness of Christ and His love. The result will be spiritual fruit (John 15:4; Gal. 5:22-23).

Our second resource is the Holy Spirit. The Holy Spirit comes to live within us the moment we receive Christ (Rom. 8:9). We are commanded to be filled with the Holy Spirit; that is, to be controlled by Him (Eph. 5:18). Being filled with or walking in the Spirit means relying on the Holy Spirit at all times.

Paul compares being filled with the Spirit with being drunk (Eph. 5:18). A drunk person's every word and action is influenced by the alcohol circulating in his bloodstream. The Spirit-filled Christian's every word and action is influenced by the Holy Spirit who lives within him.

Our third resource is God's Word. Memorizing Scripture is the key to benefiting from this resource. "Great peace have they who love Your Law, and nothing can make them stumble" (Ps. 119:165). As we tuck away verses of Scripture in our hearts and minds, we will grow spiritually (Ps. 119:11).

Memorizing and studying the Bible gives us the knowledge we need, being filled with the Holy Spirit gives us the power, and abiding in Christ is the method of righteous living. What does all this have to do with our quest to be forgiving?

Forgiveness is not our natural reaction. It is often impossible to be forgiving without God's help. Since forgiveness is basically a spiritual problem, it needs a spiritual solution. First, to be forgiving people we need to be forgiven. We discussed this foundation of a forgiving lifestyle in chapter 2.

Next, we need to focus fully on God's forgiveness of us. It is only as we begin to fathom the depths of His forgiveness that we become willing to forgive others. This should be our motivation. If we are not motivated to forgive, we do not fully understand God's forgiveness. We are being hypocritical to expect justice when we have received mercy.

But if we have accepted and understood God's forgiveness, we not only have the motivation to be forgiving, we also have the means. When we use the resources God has given us to the fullest, we can obey any command—even the ones that tell us to forgive.

When All Else Fails. . . .

At one time or another everyone has probably heard the old saying, "When all else fails, read the directions." When a manufacturer makes a product, he also writes up a list of instructions on the proper use of the product. But many of us try to figure things out for ourselves; we ignore or disregard instructions. When we do this, we take a chance that the product may not work or may be damaged by improper use.

Since God made us, He is best qualified to give us instructions on the proper use of our bodies, souls, and spirits and on the proper ways for us to relate to others. But too often we turn from God's instructions and use our own ideas. God says, "Love," but man says "Hate." God says, "Forgive," but man says, "Take revenge." When we defy God by being disobedient, we hurt ourselves and our relationships with others. (See Prov. 14:12.) Nahum wrote, "The Lord is a jealous and avenging God. . . . The Lord is slow to anger and great in power; the Lord will not leave the guilty unpunished" (Nah. 1:1,3).

Following God's instructions results in joy, wholeness, and spiritual growth. How can we obey God's commands, especially the ones that tell us to do something as difficult as forgiving others? The answer is really quite simple: we must *decide* to forgive. Forgiveness is an act of the will.

n't *Feel* Like Forgiving!"

Forgiveness is often a very painful process. If we wait till we *feel* like forgiving, we may never do it. We have to decide to forgive despite our feelings. Fortunately, our wills control our actions and our actions have the power to change our emotions. It is not hypocritical to act forgiving even if we don't feel forgiving. Obedience to God is never hypocritical. God will honor our sincere desires to live by His principles. As we determine to obey God regardless of our feelings, He often changes the feelings with which we are struggling.

The best way to handle emotions is to be primarily concerned about righteous behavior. . . . The New Testament does not devalue or disregard feeling, but subordinates it to righteous action. It is interested more in our conduct than in our reactions, more on what we *do* than on how we *feel*. To state a contemporary slogan in reverse, we could say that the New Testament approach to the emotions is: If the right thing does not feel good, do it anyway (Bert Ghezzi, *The Angry Christian,* Servant Books, p. 78).

We should not ignore or repress our God-given feelings. But we don't have to be slaves to them. We can choose to exercise our wills. We can choose to love, or we can choose to hate. We can choose to forgive, or we can choose to take revenge. We can choose to obey God, or we can choose to disobey.

Obedience always requires some demonstration that we trust God and will do as He says. Let's look at some strategies that will help us reach our goal of forgiveness. For the most part, these are areas where we can exercise our wills despite our feelings. Other than the first strategy, these suggestions are not given in any particular order; some of them may not be appropriate in every case. As we learn to exercise our wills, we must remember to depend on our three resources—for it is by faith, not self-effort, that we grow spiritually and please God (Heb. 11:6). As we depend on our resources and draw closer to

Christ, our ability to obey will increase.

Strategy 1: Resolve anger through loving confrontation

Repression of anger doesn't solve anything. It only postpones the expression of anger and can cause depression, disease, and other problems. Uncontrolled expression—whether through yelling, arguing, cursing, or destructive behavior—is not the solution either. Though this type of expression may make us feel better, at least at the time, it destroys our relationships with others and our testimony as a Christian. Controlled expression is the answer.

To feel good about expressing our anger, we need to understand two misconceptions Christians often have about anger. These two are: a Christian should never get angry and anger is always sinful. "The Bible shows us that God Himself, who is the essence of love, is fully capable of anger. In the Old Testament alone the word 'anger' appears 450 times, and 375 of those references relate to God's anger" (Lester Sumrall, *Hostility,* Thomas Nelson Publishers, p. 11). If our sinless holy God can become angry, then anger cannot always be sinful.

To determine whether our anger is sin, we should ask ourselves: *Would Jesus be angry in this situation? Will anger at this problem bring honor to Christ?* Righteous anger stems from our love of God and man. It's anger directed at the things that make God angry. More often, however, our anger is unrighteous because it springs from wounded pride or selfishness, tries to manipulate people, or is directed at something good. Unrighteous anger is sin, but righteous anger can become sin if it is not expressed appropriately.

The Scriptures give us some clear guidelines on handling anger. "Do not be quickly provoked in your spirit, for anger resides in the lap of fools. . . . A patient man has great understanding, but a quick-tempered man displays folly. . . . My dear brothers, take note of this: Everyone should be quick to listen, slow to speak and slow to become angry, for man's anger does not bring about the righteous life that God desires"

(Ecc. 7:9; Prov. 14:29; James 1:19-20).

We are also told to talk to the person who has hurt us (Luke 17:3; Matt. 18:15). When we do this we need to explain why we are angry. We should focus on the person's bothersome action without condemning or accusing. We must strive to communicate gently and lovingly and be ready to listen without becoming defensive. Perhaps the other person can open our eyes to an area in our lives that needs change. After expressing the anger, we should work together toward a solution.

"Sometimes this kind of honest confrontation is essential before we can release our resentment and extend forgiveness. We may have misunderstood the intent of the other, and this opening would give him a chance to explain himself and enable us to understand the situation from his perspective. Often simple understanding will dissolve the conflict immediately" (Creath Davis, *How to Win in a Crisis,* Zondervan, pp. 85-86).

However, there will be times when confrontation will not be possible or appropriate. In those cases, talking out our anger with another person will help us control it. We always have the option of telling God about our anger. This is what some of the psalmists did. At times God is the only One we need to talk with because it would be inappropriate to reveal our anger to others. At other times we need to talk to a trusted confidant or counselor. In addition to talking, physical exercise can also help relieve our anger.

Our spiritual resources—Jesus Christ, the Holy Spirit, and the Bible—will help us control our anger and its expression. In any event, we should resolve to leave vengeance with God. Ultimately, He is the One in control and all wrongdoers will one day answer to Him (2 Thes. 1:6-7).

Strategy 2: Practice the presence of Christ

When I put this method to work in my life, it helps me to live out many commands of Scripture. It isn't the perfect solution, still it is a method that genuinely works. When I purpose to be aware of Christ's presence, that He is with me and living in me,

I behave accordingly. I make progress and my performance is much improved. When I'm not concerned with His presence, I can easily become lax. The result: I find myself caring less, loving less, forgiving less. Qualities of Christian character are only built by ceaseless practice. (See 1 Tim. 4:7-8.)

Strategy 3: Control thought-life

I made an important discovery in those first days and nights following Diane's death. At night while I tried to sleep and at other times as well, Satan managed to vividly portray the entire episode of Diane's murder on the screen of my mind. I deplored having this scene over-amplified, but there it was each time I closed my eyes.

With God's help, I deliberately focused my thoughts on Him. As the scene would unfold, I *made* myself think on such things as are described in Philippians 4:8: "Whatever is true, whatever is noble, whatever is right, whatever is pure, whatever is lovely, whatever is admirable—if anything is excellent or praiseworthy—think about such things."

Redirecting our thoughts takes discipline and constant repetition, but it can be done. At first, I had to force myself to do this many times in a single hour. The mental battle went on for days. Then gradually these attacks became fewer and fewer, and one day I realized they were no longer haunting me.

We must carefully guard our thoughts because it is from our thoughts that our actions and attitudes spring (Rom. 12:2). If we constantly review our hurt and delight in reliving it, our hurt and anger will grow. And our actions and heart attitude will not be forgiving.

Strategy 4: Value others

Our society tends to see people as objects to be used, objects that have little or no value. But God says a single man or woman's soul is worth more than all the material goods of the world (Mark 8:36-37). When we see our offenders as people of value and as we consider their welfare instead of always selfishly looking at our own, we become freer to forgive. When we forgive others, we free them to forgive themselves.

Paul wrote, "Do nothing out of selfish ambition or vain conceit, but in humility consider others better than yourselves. Each of you should look not only to your own interests, but also to the interests of others. Your attitude should be the same as that of Christ Jesus" (Phil. 2:3-5).

Christ laid down His life for us. Can we lay down our hurt and anger for others?

Strategy 5: Remove unreasonable expectations

We often expect people to act in a certain way and when they don't, we are hurt and angry. Often the other person isn't even aware of our expectations. And until we surrender our expectations and realize people are not perfect, nor are they obligated to perform as we expect, we will have problems forgiving.

Strategy 6: Exercise understanding

Understanding underlies our forgiveness. I find it helpful to try to view my hurts through the eyes of the offenders in my life. It helps me to understand what caused them to act as they did. I can see obstacles, questions, reasons that cause delays, doubts, detours, hang-ups, and hassles I could have totally discounted from my own point of view. It keeps me from making false accusations, jumping to faulty conclusions, or being judgmental. God does this with us perfectly. I cannot do it perfectly, but it is a giant step forward. When I begin to understand, I am able to react more properly and it becomes easier to forgive.

Strategy 7: Remember only God can change people

We are responsible to God for our own attitudes and actions. But we are not responsible for the attitudes and actions of others, nor do we have the power to change others even though we may try. To be forgiving, we must learn to accept people as they are. We will probably always have some differences with others. When we do, we should attempt to resolve the problems creatively. Instead of trying to change others, we should depend on God to do the changing. We might be surprised to find Him changing us.

Strategy 8: Recognize failures

Many times when there is a conflict or a broken relationship, both people involved are somehow responsible for the problem. By refusing to forgive, we are saying all the responsibility lies with the other person. In forgiving we have to accept our share of the responsibility and that's not easy. Let's ask ourselves, *If I had acted differently, been more loving, more accessible, would this have happened? If I had not failed, or if I had succeeded more often, would I have been hurt?* When our failures have somehow contributed to the problem, we must accept this and, when necessary, ask forgiveness from God or the other person involved.

Strategy 9: Recognize our own need for forgiveness

Thinking about how often we've hurt others and how much we've appreciated receiving forgiveness should prompt us to be forgiving. We're not perfect and it's unfair of us to expect our friends and loved ones to be perfect. I find it interesting that some people have suggested that the things that bother us the most about others are often those things we dislike in ourselves. Accepting and forgiving ourselves will help with this.

Strategy 10: Deal with feelings of inferiority

Many people derive their sense of self-worth from something external: appearance, job performance, intelligence, or skill in homemaking. When this external is attacked or ignored, we feel that our self-concept and self-worth is being questioned. The hurt goes deep and it becomes difficult to forgive. It becomes easier to forgive as we realize that our self-worth is not related to anything external, but rather because we are the unique creation of God who loved and forgave us through Christ.

Strategy 11: Eliminate conditions

"I could forgive if he'd say he's sorry." "I'd forgive her if she said she'd learned her lesson." "If he tells the truth, I'll forgive."

How many times have we said or heard statements like this? Whenever we say, "I'll forgive if. . . ." we are placing a condition on our forgiveness. In a sense, we're making the offender earn his forgiveness. But "forgiveness" is a gift. A gift does not depend on the nature of the receiver but on the giver. A gift is not given to one who has earned it—then it becomes a payment" (David Augsburger, *Be All You Can Be!* Choice Books, p. 120).

Strategy 12: Verbalize forgiveness as a goal

When we're having problems following through with a project or behavior, it often helps to share our desire with a friend or two. When we're aware that others know of our desire and intent, it challenges us to keep with it. If we tell a trusted friend or two that we truly desire to be forgiving, they will be there to support us when we stumble. If we tell God we desire to be forgiving, He will give us the opportunities to learn how and the strength to succeed.

Strategy 13: Eat, sleep, and exercise

Since we tend to react best to adverse situations when we feel physically fit, eating properly and getting the right amount of sleep and exercise will also help.

Strategy 14: Take the eternal view

Many of our conflicts and problems result from temporal things: Money, position, power, and possessions. To succeed in forgiving, we need to think in terms of eternity. Will this offense or this problem matter in eternity? If not, why should we allow it to affect us now? When we focus on our hurts, our vision is blurred to the good things in our lives. But when we focus on eternity, we see clearly which things really have lasting value. With eternity in view, it's easier to forgive temporal problems.

Strategy 15: Realize limitations
During a conversation with the wife of a nationally known minister, she said had she been faced with my situation, she didn't know if she would have been able to forgive. I assured her she wouldn't know how she would react till she was in that situation. God would not give her the grace to handle something till she was actually faced with handling it.

Some of us are afraid to adopt a forgiving lifestyle because we think something will come along that we will never be able to forgive. This is not an unreasonable fear, because it is not humanly possible for us to practice total forgiveness perfectly. But as we admit this to God, He will give us the strength to accomplish what we cannot do in our own strength.

Can We Forgive the Unrepentant?
Some people teach we cannot and should not forgive till our offenders ask for our forgiveness and promise to change their ways. The reasoning goes something like this: if I forgive someone who has not yet repented, I will be encouraging that person to continue to sin against me.

But I don't believe Christ would have us store up our anger and hurt feelings till our offenders decide to seek forgiveness. That may never happen. We would then be bound forever by our hate and bitterness. For our own health and our own spiritual growth, we should always forgive from the heart—whether or not our offender seeks our forgiveness. God didn't wait for us to seek His forgiveness (1 Cor. 5:8).

Can a person who offends us, supposedly repents, and then goes on to offend us several more times in the same day, be truly repentant? Maybe. Maybe not. Forgiveness is somewhat easier when we know the offender has truly changed his or her ways, but it becomes hard when we know we will be hurt in the same way again and again.

There are two steps to forgiveness. The first is a change in heart attitude in which the person offended is not condoning the wrong, but decides holding a grudge won't do anyone any good. This positive heart attitude is essential for the success of the second step, which is reconciliation. Lasting reconciliation is impossible unless the attitude of the offended changes. But a change in his attitude is possible even if the two are never reconciled. In other words, we can forgive someone who has not repented. But our forgiveness is no guarantee that the offender will change or that we will ever be reconciled. Until we are reconciled, forgiveness is not complete. (We will deal further with this in chapter 9.)

God has already provided forgiveness for us. But our reconciliation with God does not actually take place until we seek God's forgiveness. Similarly, when we change our attitude toward our offender there is the possibility of reconciliation. But reconciliation does not actually happen until our offender accepts our forgiveness.

Forgiving through Prayer

Our actual act of forgiving another can best be accomplished through prayer. The following prayer may be helpful:

> *Dear Lord, as an act of my will I will forgive* _____*for*_____. *I do not feel like forgiving, but I am choosing to follow Your commands. Please forgive my unwillingness to forgive, for that is sin. Cleanse me of anger, bitterness, resentment, and any of the other fruit of unforgiveness. Please help me to truly begin to love my offender. Help me to forgive as You have forgiven me.*

If we trust that forgiving is God's best for us, if we pray this or a similar prayer in faith as an act of obedience, we can expect God to empower us to do what we can't do on our own. Let's take some time to forgive each individual and each action we may have on the list we compiled in chapters 6 and 7.

Forgiving Multiple or Repeated Offenses

One good friend of mine said that to forgive a great big event in one's life once and for all, such as Diane's murder, is quite different from forgiving a smaller offense over and over again. I agree. This is a difficult situation to handle. An impossible one without God's help.

When we are first learning to forgive, we can get overwhelmed as we think of every wrong deed that's ever been committed against us and our family. We think, "I can't forgive all this." That's true. We may not be able to forgive everything that ever happened to us all at once. Forgiveness is often a process.

Sandra "Judy" Hampton, the former Judy Warren, came to the nation's attention in the mid 1950s after her stepmother blinded Judy by pressing her thumbs against Judy's eyes. Several years after this happened, Judy was confronted with the truth of God's Word that as a Christian, God expected her to forgive. At first, she could not forgive her stepmother, but she was able to forgive the welfare department for denying her permission to have sight-saving surgery. She asked the Lord to help her with her unforgiveness toward her stepmother. After several years, she discovered she had forgiven.

"It had not happened overnight and it had not been easy," Judy writes, "but it was a fact that I had forgiven her. It was as if the Lord had done emotional surgery on me, and cut away any trace of unforgiveness. I know it was a miracle that would not have been possible except through the Lord" (Sandra Judy Hampton with Lee Hultquist, *Whatever Happened to Judy?* Logos International, pp. 154-155).

Dr. Richard P. Walters, staff psychologist at the Pine Rest Christian Hospital in Grand Rapids, Michigan suggests the following when we have multiple offenses to forgive:

- Begin by forgiving what you can.
- Pray for a willingness to forgive the rest.
- As you can, forgive the rest of those matters.
- Don't be surprised to remember more offenses. Deal with them one by one.

How Long Does Forgiveness Take?

When Rev. Brown* returned from his two-week vacation, he could sense that something was wrong. The minutes from a recent church board meeting said all staff positions and goals had been reevaluated.

Rev. Brown thought back to the time two years before when he had been hired as the minister of education. He had interviewed for one job, but had been offered this one. Even though Rev. Brown had no more background in Christian education than the average seminary graduate, he had decided to accept the job and the challenge.

Several times since his hiring, the church board had given him a feeling that they weren't happy with his job performance. "But they never really spelled it out," he says. "They never told me what was wrong or what needed to be changed. I worked under the assumption that as long as the senior minister wasn't making any major criticisms, that as long as I satisfied him, everything was OK."

But it wasn't. At 9 A.M. on the Monday after Rev. Brown returned from vacation, the senior minister told him the church board had fired him. Without warning. Without notice. Understandably, Rev. Brown was hurt and angry. Time and time again he found himself struggling with bitter, vengeful thoughts. To help resolve his feelings, he had conferences with the senior minister and church board. He expressed his hurt to individual board members. He prayed. Finally, he felt he had forgiven those involved.

About five months after the incident, after he had taken a

---

*Not his real name.

pastorate in another town, Rev. Brown went to a conference and ran into two of the individuals who had hurt him so much. Bitterness and anger boiled up within him. When he got back home from the conference, he found he was spending a lot of time thinking about his hurt and he couldn't concentrate.

Rev. Brown checked into a motel one afternoon and spent the next 24 hours reading the Bible and other materials on forgiveness, meditating, praying, and fasting. This experience was a key in breaking the power of unforgiveness in his life.

As he looks back on his experience, it was nearly 6 months before he had truly forgiven and almost 10 months before he felt he had resolved his hurt and resumed a normal life. Forgiveness for Rev. Brown was a process.

For Ella Jo Sadler forgiveness also took time. In her book *Murder in the Afternoon,* she relates how 2 youths murdered her father and her best friend and attempted to murder her and her mother simply because the youths wanted to steal their car. It was 11 years after the incident before Mrs. Sadler could say she had forgiven those involved (Zondervan, pp. 168-169).

For some, forgiveness is a struggle that takes time. For others it occurs right away. I have been asked several times to explain the steps I took in order to forgive Diane's murderer. I can't do that because forgiveness was my immediate reaction. This is also true of my husband and two sons. I cannot remember a time when we all sat down and decided, "To hold hostility toward our daughter's killer is not doing us any good. This is what we must do to forgive." The forgiveness was simply there and we believe that was a miracle. This doesn't mean that I'm special or my family is special, or even that we're unique.

Corrie ten Boom's meeting with a former guard from the Nazi Concentration Camp at Ravensbruck is another example of immediate forgiveness. She had been speaking about forgiveness in a German church. After the service, the guard approached her and asked her to forgive him. Corrie didn't feel like forgiving, but she chose to forgive.

She reflects, "And so woodenly, mechanically, I thrust my hand into the one stretched out to me. And as I did, an incredible thing took place. The current started in my shoulder, raced down my arm, sprang into our joined hands. And then this healing warmth seemed to flood my whole being, bringing tears to my eyes.

"'I forgive you brother,' I cried. 'With all my heart'" (Corrie ten Boom with Jamie Buckingham, *Tramp for the Lord,* Revell, p. 57).

Forgiveness can be immediate or it can be a long hard struggle. I'm not sure why God chooses to work differently in different people's lives. I suspect it may have something to do with our family backgrounds, temperaments, personalities, spiritual maturity, and even the type of offenses involved.

How long does it take to forgive? There's no pat answer. For some it may be immediate. For some it may take months or years. But it can happen and it's worth the time spent.

Forgiveness Means . . . .

Forgiveness means our emotional response to our offender has changed from negative to positive.

Forgiveness means we transfer the responsibility for any punishment to God.

Forgiveness means we never give up on our offender "as a human being, never deem him hopeless, never deprive him of a chance to make it up to [us]" (Phyllis Reynolds Naylor, "What It Means to Forgive," *Reach,* April 1981, p. 9).

Forgiveness does not mean we try to teach the offender a lesson first before forgiving, or that we demand repayment, that we act like it never happened, or that the offense did not hurt.

Forgiveness does not mean there will be no consequences, no cost to be paid, no loss to bear. Because I forgave Tom, Diane's life was not restored. Because Judy forgave, her eyesight did not return, nor did Rev. Brown get his job back when he forgave. Whenever there is an offense there will be a cost to be paid, a loss to bear. When the offender is punished or is required to bear the loss, that is justice. But when the offended bears the loss, abstains from personal vengeance, and transfers any responsibility for punishment to God, that is forgiveness.

I Know I've Forgiven When . . . .

I no longer have the fruit of unforgiveness in my life.

I can talk about my offense without getting angry, resentful, or bitter.

I can talk about my offender without getting a knot in my stomach.

I can wish my offender good.

I can look my offender in the eye with true and honest love in my heart.

I can revisit the scene of the event without having a negative reaction.

I can do good to those who have hurt me.

I can be joyful.

9
Now What?

Finally, brothers, whatever is true, whatever is noble, whatever is right, whatever is pure, whatever is lovely, whatever is admirable—if anything is excellent or praiseworthy—think about such things (Phil. 4:8).

The young man felt that life was passing him by. He considered every day he was out in his father's fields sweating and working, a day lost to fun and laughter. He became resentful. He hated his life, his work, and his father. So he began to plan and plot.

His dad was rich. He knew that. How many times had his father told him that one day part of all the land and wealth would be his own? He looked around him. Why wait till he was too old to enjoy what was rightfully his? If he could have his inheritance now, then he could really begin to live. He wouldn't have to work. He could do whatever he wanted. So one day he said, "Father, give me my share of the estate."

His father did as he was asked. Not long after that, the young man gathered his belongings and headed for a distant land where he wasted his money in wild living.

When a severe famine swept the land, the young man became so hungry he was forced to get a job feeding a rich man's pigs. He was so poor and so hungry even the pig's food looked appealing. As he gazed at the food, he remembered better times, times when he lived with his father and there was always plenty of appetizing food to eat. He came to his senses.

"How many of my father's hired men have food to spare, and here I am starving to death! I will set out and go back to my father and say to him: 'Father, I have sinned against heaven and against you. I am no longer worthy to be called your son; make me like one of your hired men.'" He immediately left his job with the pigs and headed home.

While the young man was still a long way from his father's house, his father saw him. With an aching and longing heart, the father had been watching daily for the return of his son. When he finally saw him, he was filled with compassion and ran to his son, threw his arms around him, and kissed him.

During the long walk, the son had been mentally rehearsing for this moment. Now the words tumbled out. "Father, I have sinned against heaven and against you. I am no longer worthy to be called your son."

But it was as if the father hadn't even heard. He turned to his servants standing by and said, "Quick! Bring the best robe and put it on him. Put a ring on his finger and sandals on his feet. Bring the fattened calf and kill it. Let's have a feast and celebrate. For this son of mine was dead and is alive again; he was lost and is found."

The forgiving father and his prodigal son were reconciled. (See Luke 15:11-24.)

What Is Reconciliation?

Reconciliation means to harmonize or settle a disagreement, to reunite, to make peace, to agree, to restore to fellowship and confidence. Whenever an offense, a disagreement, a hurt has separated two people, reconciliation is the proof that forgiveness has been given and accepted.

Generally speaking, as Christians we should initiate reconciliation by going to our offenders in private. If our offenders are fellow believers, we do this to preserve the unity of the body of Christ. "He who covers over an offense promotes love" (Prov. 17:9). Peter writes, "Above all, love each other deeply because love covers over a multitude of sins" (1 Peter 4:8). (See Matt. 18:15; Eph. 4:3; 2 Cor. 2:5-11.) If our offenders are not believers, we can use this as an opportunity to demonstrate God's love and forgiveness (2 Cor. 5:11-21).

I hesitate to say we can and should *always* initiate reconciliation, for in some situations this is not possible or appropriate. Let's look at some of these special situations.

What If . . . .

Jane grew up hating her father for beating and belittling her. He had never hugged or kissed her or even said he cared. When Jane became a Christian in her early 20s, God convicted her of her attitude toward her father. Little by little, God chipped away at her hate, hurt, and anger. Now she can truthfully say she has forgiven her father, and she would dearly love to tell him that, but it's impossible. Several years ago Jane's father died.

When our offenders are dead, it is impossible to initiate reconciliation. But it is possible to talk out our feelings with God, and when necessary, to talk with a trusted counselor or confidant. They can help us resolve any lingering anger, guilt, and bitterness and put the situation in perspective.

* * *

About three months before Diane's death, she had written to my husband Bob and me from California requesting that we leave her alone. She cut the lines of communication between us, disrupting our relationship. We knew we could not be reconciled with our daughter till she had a change of attitude. I suppose we could have tried to force her to communicate with us, but we decided it would be best to honor her request. We waited, leaving the situation in God's hands. Miraculously, two weeks later Diane showed up at our summer home in Michigan. Like the prodigal son, she had had a change in attitude and we were able to be reconciled. Similarly, when our offenders refuse to hear us or talk with us, it's impossible to discuss reconciliation. But we can wait and pray, asking God to give our offenders a desire to communicate with us.

* * *

Shortly after hearing the news of Diane's death, we forgave Diane's assailant. But who was he? And where was he? We didn't know until three years later, and until we knew his whereabouts we could not even begin to initiate reconciliation. When we don't know our offenders' whereabouts, it's impossible to initiate reconciliation—at least for the moment. But we can wait and pray, asking God to help us locate our offenders. We can leave the matter in His hands.

* * *

Sometimes when we're offended it's not clear who's right and who's wrong. It can even be questionable that an offense actually occurred. Remember Rev. Brown from the last chapter? He was hurt deeply by the way his church board handled his firing. But the board members felt they were within their rights to make that decision. They felt they had done no wrong. Did Rev. Brown tell the board members he had forgiven them?

He explains, "When I say, 'I forgive you' that means you've done something wrong and that's a judgment on my part. Because the board felt they had done no wrong, for me to go to the board and tell them I'd forgiven them would have been a very prideful act and it would have been accepted as such. There would have been no value in telling them I'd forgiven them, because in their eyes they hadn't done anything wrong."

If we're inadvertently hurt, like Rev. Brown, or if we are offended because we're overly sensitive, because our expectations aren't being met, or because we're feeling neglected or envious, we may not have actually separated from our offenders. In fact, the other persons may be totally unaware we've been offended. Going to them to say, "I forgive you," may sound judgmental and superior. It could erect a barrier and prevent further communication.

Instead, we could say, "I feel angry because . . . ." or "I felt hurt when . . . ." Then we are not placing blame on the other; we're shifting the focus to ourselves: to our needs, impressions, and feelings. Hopefully, the other persons will feel free to discuss the situation. Rev. Brown expressed his hurt this way, and even though he had forgiven, he didn't think it appropriate to mention it.

* * *

Two other areas where it may not be appropriate to initiate reconciliation is when we are offended by something someone does to one of our loved ones or when we are "offended" by someone's good qualities. In the first case, the problem does not directly concern us and we could complicate the situation by stepping into it. In the second case, the main problem lies with us, not with others. We may hurt the other person by admitting our resentment and envy.

If we are having problems deciding whether to initiate reconciliation, we should ask ourselves: *Am I avoiding this person, or refusing to talk to him whereas before I had enjoyed his fellowship? Is there a barrier in our relationship, a coldness or distance that wasn't there before?* If so, then it's probably a good idea to seek reconciliation.

Initiating Reconciliation

The pattern for initiating reconciliation found in Scripture is for a private, one-on-one meeting. "If your brother sins against you, go and show him his fault, just between the two of you" (Matt. 18:15). "Brothers, if someone is caught in a sin, you who are spiritual should restore him gently. But watch yourself, or you also may be tempted" (Gal. 6:1). This principle refers to our relationships with fellow believers. But a personal meeting is also best when we are dealing with non-believers.

Common sense tells us to choose a convenient time and place for this meeting. In some cases, it might be a good idea to set up the time and place in advance.

When our offenders are not available for a personal meeting, a letter or phone call may work, but we have to be careful when we use these means. It is so easy for letters and phone calls to be misinterpreted. If we have to use these means, we may want to write a letter first and then follow up with a phone call.

During our meeting we should be honest and explain how the person's behavior affected us. We should assure our offenders we have forgiven them and want the relationship to continue. Dr. Richard P. Walters suggests we also explain why we wanted to share our feelings with our offender. "Give the message, 'You as a person are worthwhile,' with no strings attached," he explains. "If that isn't true, you haven't forgiven."

We should be prepared to listen. We may also need to ask for forgiveness for our mistakes or failures which contributed to the situation.

When our offenders refuse our forgiveness or refuse to admit wrong and show no interest in the relationship, we cannot force them to change. But we've fulfilled our responsibility and we can expect God to work in our offenders' lives.

I've heard it said that we should not tell someone we've forgiven him or her till that person repents and asks for our forgiveness. If we initiate reconciliation, then we are encouraging that person to continue to do wrong. But this kind of forgiveness troubles me. First, if God had decided to keep quiet about His forgiveness until we repented, none of us would be Christians now. If God's kindness can lead to our repentance, couldn't our kindness lead to our offender's repentance? (Rom. 2:4; 5:8)

Second, in many cases it wouldn't be fair for us to expect our offenders to do all the repenting or changing. In interpersonal relationships there are very few situations where one person is totally wrong and the other person is the innocent victim. Both people, to some degree or another, are usually at fault. For us to refuse to lovingly confront until the other person changes is to ignore our part in the problem.

Of course, no matter how hard we may try to be reconciled, we have no guarantee of success. What are our options then?

If the situation is one in which our offenders claim to be Christians and are clearly violating God's Law, yet refuse to repent, we may want to use God's plan for church discipline. (For guidelines, see Matt. 18:15-17; Gal. 6:1-2; 1 Cor. 5:11; 6:1-5; 1 Tim. 5:19-20; 2 Cor. 2:5-11.) Church discipline, however, is only to be administered when the offense is definitely sin. In most other cases, all we can do is wait and pray.

Whether or not our offenders are Christians, we must assure them of our continued love and forgiveness because we believe they have value and worth. But we should make it clear we are not condoning their offense in any way.

We should keep in mind that we could someday be guilty of the same offense and as ambassadors for Christ our forgiveness and attempts at reconciliation are a reflection on Him.

When we are not reconciled with our offenders, forgiveness is not complete. But we cannot be held responsible for the actions of others. We're only responsible for our own actions. By changing our attitudes and attempting to initiate reconciliation, we've fulfilled our obligation.

Guarding Against the Return of Bitter Fruit

Forgetting is a part of forgiving. Whether or not we are reconciled with our offenders, forgetting must follow forgiveness in order to guard against the return of anger and bitterness.

Forgetting, according to David Augsburger, is "not a case of holy amnesia which erases the past. No, instead it is the experience of healing which draws the poison from the wound. You may recall the hurt, but you will not relive it! No constant reviewing, no rehashing of the old hurt, no going back to sit on the old gravestones where past grievances lie buried. True, the hornet of memory may fly again, but forgiveness has drawn its sting. The curse is gone. The memory is powerless to arouse or anger. . . . Forgiveness restores the present, heals for the future, and releases us from the past" *(The Freedom of Forgiveness,* Moody Press, p. 39).

Practically speaking, what does it mean to forget?

• Forgetting means not keeping a record of the wrong or filing away evidence for future use (1 Cor. 13:5).

• Forgetting means refusing to dwell on the event or to talk about it every chance we get (Phil. 4:8-9; Prov. 17:9).

• Forgetting means looking ahead to the future (Phil. 3:13).

• Forgetting means saying good things about our offenders and doing helpful deeds for them (Luke 6:27-28; Rom. 12:20).

• Forgetting means allowing God to erase our painful memories (Gen. 41:51).

Someone has said that to forgive and not forget is simply to bury the hatchet with the handle sticking out. When we do that, the handle will always be there to draw our attention to the hatchet, and on occasion, to trip us.

During Rev. Brown's 24-hour period of fasting, prayer, and Bible study, God showed him a basic lesson about forgiveness: thanking God for the lessons learned through the experience is an antidote for bitter thoughts.

"As soon as I thought bitter thoughts, I thanked God for the lessons I had learned and for my spiritual growth," he says. "Within two to three weeks I had no trouble with bitter thoughts."

Thanksgiving is a sign we trust that God is really in control of our lives and the lives of all the others that touch us. Many times it will be hard to understand why God allows something and we're not going to feel like thanking Him. But even if we don't feel like it, we can do it as an act of our will. We are commanded to give thanks just like we are commanded to forgive. "Give thanks in all circumstances, for this is God's will for you in Christ Jesus" (1 Thes. 5:18).

Notice this verse doesn't say, "Give thanks *for* all circumstances," but *"in* all circumstances." There is a difference. For example, I personally couldn't thank God *for* the circumstances surrounding Diane's death, but I could and did thank Him *in* the circumstances, knowing He works all things together for good (Rom. 8:28).

Ken Poure, a speaker at family conferences throughout the nation, has said that the time lapse between an adverse circumstance and our giving thanks to God indicates our spiritual maturity. If it is only moments, then we are spiritual. If it is 15 minutes to an hour, we are growing. But if it is an hour to several days, then he says, we're in trouble spiritually (Tim LaHaye, *How to Win Over Depression,* Zondervan, p. 211).

Praying for our offender—for his salvation if he is not a Christian and for blessings—will help our attitude toward our offender. It's impossible to sincerely pray for someone and at the same time hate or be resentful toward him (Matt. 5:44; Luke 6:28).

Put on Love

When we have forgiven, our offenders and those around us will know it by our attitude and actions. What better way is there to demonstrate forgiveness than by our love?

If we have been reconciled to our offenders, loving may come easily. But if we are not reconciled, loving can be very difficult. "Our own needs, pains, and griefs [will] scream for our undivided attention. Yet giving in would do nothing but hurt us, for often hearing only comes when we get our minds off ourselves and show concern for others and their cares and interests" (Joni Eareckson and Steve Estes, *A Step Further,* Zondervan, p. 90). Loving can be the very thing that persuades our offenders we're sincere and challenges them to change.

What is love? Biblical love is active; it's not necessarily a warm feeling or pleasant emotion.

> Christian love is the decision of your will to act in a concerned, responsible way toward another whether you like him or not. Love is not an emotion that just comes naturally, it's an action that comes from an inner decision to follow Jesus Christ's way of helpful, self-forgetful, purposeful compassion (David Augsburger, *Be All You Can Be!* Choice Books, p. 95).

The Apostle Paul penned the best description of love. "Love is very patient and kind, never jealous or envious, never boastful or proud, never haughty or selfish or rude. Love does not demand its own way. It is not irritable or touchy. It does not hold grudges and will hardly even notice when others do it wrong. It is never glad about injustice, but rejoices whenever truth wins out. If you love someone you will be loyal to him no matter what the cost. You will always believe in him, always expect the best of him, and always stand your ground in defending him (1 Cor. 13:4-7, LB).

We are exhorted to put on love. "Therefore, as God's chosen people, holy and dearly loved, clothe yourselves with compassion, kindness, humility, gentleness, and patience. Bear with each other and forgive whatever grievances you may have against one another. Forgive as the Lord forgave you. And over all these virtues put on love, which binds them all together in perfect unity" (Col. 3:12-14).

Love, which is the supreme grace, covers a multitude of sins (1 Peter 4:8). This grace must rest on our compassion, kindness, humility, gentleness, and patience. Love is like the outer garment, the top layer of clothing which completes and keeps together all the rest. Without putting on love, all the other virtues would be loose, disconnected, and unbalanced. Love binds them all together so they can't slip out of place.

This is not optional—for love is the required outer garment

of our lives. But it will not fit properly if lying underneath are evil things which we have not "put off." Love adjusts and adheres only to healthy spiritual attitudes, then our spiritual clothing fits beautifully and brings glory and honor to Jesus Christ (Rom. 13:14; Col. 3:9-10).

10
Creating an Environment for Forgiveness

> Make sure that nobody pays back wrong for wrong,
> but always try to be kind to each other and to
> everyone else. Be joyful always; pray continually;
> give thanks in all circumstances, for this is God's will
> for you in Christ Jesus (1 Thes. 5:15-18).

The autumn air was fresh and the sun was shining with a warm softness, accentuating the red, orange, yellow, and gold leaves in the trees. It was one of those days when it feels good to be alive and my spirit was soaring as I walked into our local restaurant for an early morning breakfast.

Another customer sat at the table next to me. "Good morning!" the waitress said pleasantly.

"What's good about it?" the customer snapped. Then she released a series of complaints about life in general. It had turned cold too soon; she felt rotten; she hated her boss; prices were too high; and the menu had nothing tasty listed. She settled for a cup of black coffee. Probably without realizing it, she was creating an uncomfortable environment in that restaurant.

That incident made me realize how our attitudes can create

either a pleasant or unpleasant environment for those around us. Our attitudes can set the tone in our homes and churches. Our attitudes, whether good or bad, can rub off onto others, just as the attitudes of others can rub off onto us. Because we can control our attitudes, we have the ability to create an environment where forgiveness flows freely or one where revenge, hatred, and distrust reign. Which will we choose?

Making Forgiveness Our Goal

First, to develop a forgiving lifestyle we must make forgiveness our goal. Making forgiveness a way of life is similar to continually handing our anxieties to the Lord (Phil. 4:6). Forgiveness as a lifestyle can be like praying without ceasing (1 Thes. 5:17). And it can be likened to the continuous cleansing of our sin through Christ's blood (1 John 1:9).

We can live in forgiveness continually, but we may hesitate to say that we will. The thought of that can overwhelm us. Let's look at it another way. Can we resolve to be forgiving for today? Since a forgiving lifestyle is directly tied to our Christian walk, I've found the following habit helpful.

For the past dozen years or so, as soon as I awake I ask God to cleanse my heart from all sin through Christ's precious blood so that I may be clean and whole *for this day:* not for tomorrow, or next month, or yesterday, but for *today.* I confess any known sins and ask God to cleanse me of any secret sins. I claim the promise of 1 John 1:9: "If we confess our sins, He is faithful and just and will forgive us our sins and purify us from all unrighteousness."

Next, I ask God to renew my mind so my thinking will be clear and Holy Spirit controlled *for today:* not for tomorrow, or next week, but for *now.* There is much in this world vying for my attention and I want my mind set on Christ for today. I also claim these promises from Scripture: "You will keep in perfect peace him whose mind is steadfast, because he trusts in You" (Isa. 26:3). "Commit thy works unto the Lord, and thy thoughts shall be established" (Prov. 16:3, KJV). "And the peace of God, which transcends all understanding, will guard your hearts and your minds in Christ Jesus" (Phil. 4:7).

Last, I ask God to fill me with His Holy Spirit, so I may be empowered and adequate in Him to be His person *for this day*. With my sins cleansed, there is nothing hindering the Holy Spirit from controlling my thoughts and actions.

Putting this formula into daily practice, even though I err often, has helped me in actually living the Christian life on a day-to-day basis. I am not overwhelmed as I think of living my whole life for Christ. I am living and forgiving for Him one day at a time. This practice makes me conscious of God's presence and, as a result, I am much more sensitive to sin and unhealthy attitudes. When I do fail, the Holy Spirit instantly nudges me and I go to God for forgiveness and then get right on with my living for Him.

My 95-year-old mother also adopted this formula for her life about the same time I did. She says she has grown more in Christ over the past dozen years than at any other period in her life. That's a fantastic testimonial for its workability in one's life.

But whether you choose to follow this routine or a similar one, an important part of developing a forgiving lifestyle is to turn your thinking toward God when starting each day. You will be more apt to react appropriately when you are daily abiding in Christ and conscious of His presence.

The Power of a Forgiving Environment

Four months after Johnnie's 15-year-old son Larry ran away from home, Johnnie said the Lord began to impress on her that she should take the full blame for the things that had gone wrong in her family.

"It had been so easy for me to blame my husband for not being the father I thought he should have been," she explains. "It was easy to blame my son for not measuring up. He was on drugs; he had quit school. I couldn't accept that. I had just seen his failures, and somehow hadn't seen the part I had played in the problem. When God began to show me my part in it, there was no room for looking at either of their failures."

Miraculously, Johnnie says, she was not only able to forgive Larry but she knew it was necessary for her to ask him for forgiveness. She decided to write him a letter, asking him to forgive everything she had done badly—for the times she had failed to love him and for the things she had neglected to do.

"I asked the Lord as I wrote to make it clear that I was assuming the blame," she recalls. "I didn't even want to inadvertently pass more guilt on to him."

She poured her heart into the letter even though she had no address for her son and no guarantee he'd ever read it. She gave the letter to one of Larry's friends, asking him to pass it along. "I knew God was going to have to take that letter and get it to him," she says.

Another four months went by. Then one evening her son showed up at her front door with three of his friends.

"We were entertaining four other couples for dinner," Johnnie recalls. "The way Larry looked that night is etched in my mind. At first, I was shocked and dismayed at his appearance. He was gaunt. His 6'2" frame only carried about 120 pounds. His naturally curly hair was down to his shoulders and he had dyed it red. But even though I knew my dinner guests were there, it was like the Lord put blinders on me and I was able to concentrate on my son. I was able to act perfectly natural. I didn't know how long he was going to stay and when he left, if I'd ever see him again."

During the 20-minute visit, Johnnie hugged her son 2 or 3 times and told him how glad she was to see him. When he asked to borrow $20, she freely gave it to him.

"I knew it would probably go to drugs," she says, "but the Lord seemed to say, 'You're going to have to trust Me for this. I have deeper things going on here.'"

Before Larry and his friends left, Johnnie offered them all some dessert, hugged each of them, and told them she cared.

It was 18 months before Johnnie's son returned.

"He moved in with some fellows in an awful part of town in a house filled with other runaways and kids with problems. This was really the beginning of my wooing him with unconditional love and showing him that my forgiveness wasn't just on paper."

When Johnnie would go to the house to visit her son, if he came to the door at all, he would refuse to let her inside.

"He would be cold and indifferent and it was clear I was unwanted.

"I got bold as I went along," she remembers. "I knew my love couldn't be passive. I'd practically have to push myself into the house and assert authority. The kids weren't friendly to me, but they would respect me.

"Little by little, the Lord began to deal with Larry allowing him to see things that shocked and distressed him and convinced him that type of lifestyle wasn't for him. At my end, the Lord was giving me the strength to love my son unconditionally."

Finally, her son started to go with Johnnie when she came to visit.

"The Lord seemed to say to me, 'You have to show him love in a way that will convince him.' I'd take him to the nicest restaurants. For awhile he wouldn't even order, or if he did, he'd just look at the food.

"Many times I'd just sit there and weep. But little by little we opened up to each other.

"As we were having these talks over dinner, he'd say, 'Mom, you have nothing to be ashamed of,' or 'That is not your fault.' As I got some of these things off my chest, he was able to start taking some of the blame for his problems."

For two years Larry lived in the house, and for two years Johnnie frequently visited him. She also continued to write letters, discussing the times she felt she had failed him.

"We had a lot of making up to do. I had to step back and allow the relationship to slowly rebuild."

Gradually, Johnnie could see God working in her son's life. He moved from the house and he fell in love with a woman, who later became his wife. Nine years after Johnnie wrote her original letter, Larry was convinced of the reality of Jesus Christ and received him as his Saviour. Today, Larry holds a steady job, is married and the father of a son, and most of all, is reconciled with his family.

Ingredients of a Forgiving Lifestyle

Several attitudes are necessary for us to forgive specific incidents. We've referred to several of these already. There's faith, trust, honesty, and understanding. There's kindness, joy, and thankfulness. There's humility and self-love. Of course, love *is* the all important ingredient. The key to creating an environment of forgiveness or cultivating a forgiving lifestyle is to concentrate on making these attitudes a daily part of our lives.

We can see many of these attitudes at work in Johnnie's experience. First, Johnnie constantly depended on God to work in her son's life and in her own. She depended on God for guidance and for the divine strength to offer her son unconditional love and acceptance.

When Johnnie stopped blaming others, recognized her failures, and asked for her son's forgiveness, she had torn down a very large barrier in their relationship. Often when we consider forgiving someone else, we are concentrating on their wrong and can be blind to our wrongs. If we ignore our wrongs, offering forgiveness can become an act of judgment or an exercise in superiority. We must always keep in mind our imperfections and be ready to ask for forgiveness when necessary.

Johnnie practiced forbearance. Forbearance means to refrain or hold back, to be patient or self-controlled, to endure, to bear or put up with, to suffer, to permit. Ephesians 4:2 commands us to bear with one another in love. "To 'bear with one another,' then," writes Dr. Gene Getz, "means being patient with each other's weaknesses" *(Building Up One Another,* Victor Books, p. 92). Forbearance is not a "grin and bear it" type reaction while we're knotted up inside, or gritting our teeth and saying, "I'm going to love this person if it kills me." Forbearance is a patient acceptance of people because we recognize we're all imperfect, we're all in various stages of emotional and spiritual growth, and God loves us all equally. A person who forbears is not touchy and will not easily take offense.

Since Johnnie did not have the power to change her son, she was left with two options: to accept him or to reject him. This is the choice all of us have. If we really wish to promote forgiveness, we must accept others. In fact, Scripture commands that we accept others. "Accept him whose faith is weak, without passing judgment on disputable matters. . . . accept one another, then, just as Christ accepted you, in order to bring praise to God" (Rom. 14:1; 15:7).

Many Christians fear that accepting another means ignoring biblical standards. This is not true. Biblical acceptance of another does not imply approval of undesirable behavior, a lowering of our standards, or even our total agreement with the other person. Acceptance does mean we recognize another's right to disagree with us. Acceptance means we lay aside prejudice and refuse to play favorites (Rom. 12:16; James 2:1). Acceptance does not say, "Become like me and then I will accept you." Acceptance does not demand change, but it encourages growth. And mostly, acceptance sees people and loves them as God does.

Whenever our acceptance of others is based on our own personal standards or taste, or on an extra-biblical list of do's and don'ts, we are guilty of judging. Perhaps Johnnie had been guilty of this before her son left home. "Judging takes many forms: knocking, mudslinging, gossip, jumping to conclusions, backbiting, slandering, caustically criticizing. By judging, we . . . usurp the prerogative of God who alone knows all the facts" (Leslie B. Flynn, *Great Church Fights,* Victor Books, p. 110).

We are warned against judging our fellow believers. Jesus said, "Do not judge, or you too will be judged. For in the same way you judge others, you will be judged, and with the measure you use, it will be measured to you" (Matt. 7:1-2).

Pauls asks, "You, then, why do you judge your brother? Or why do you look down on your brother? For we will all stand before God's judgment seat. It is written: 'As surely as I live,' says the Lord, 'every knee will bow before Me; every tongue will confess to God.' So then, each of us will give an account of himself to God. Therefore, let us stop passing judgment on one another" (Rom. 14:10-13).

Paul also tells us not to judge nonbelievers. "What business is it of mine to judge those outside the church? God will judge those outside" (1 Cor. 5:12-13).

In a sense, judging is playing God, but because we are not His equals and have extremely limited viewpoints, we will never know the whole story behind an act. We have no foolproof method of assessing motives. Our emotions color our own motives.*

Because we are not qualified to be judges, God relieves us of this responsibility by promising to avenge. "I will repay," He says (Rom. 12:19). I think of it this way: vengeance is God's department, so why should I monkey around with it? Johnnie could have been tempted to take matters into her own hands and somehow have punished her son for his wrong. Instead, she depended on God to work and by doing that was promoting an environment of forgiveness.

Johnnie made her forgiveness and love active and visible. It started with her first letter and continued the night her son dropped in on her unexpectedly. She hugged him; she hugged his friends; she offered them food; she loaned them money. She was living her love and forgiveness when she visited her son at the house and took him to the finest restaurants in town. She showed she was sincere by her persistence.

Adding these attitudes to our lives will help us create an

---

*We are allowed to direct and guide a Christian brother or sister, but only if we are sure the person is really breaking one of God's laws and if we ourselves are spiritual (Gal. 6:1; Col. 3:16; Rom. 15:14).

environment of forgiveness between friends, and in our marriages, our homes, and our churches. Actually, it boils down to living and loving like Christ. It is Christ's nature to forgive. He doesn't have to wait until He's in the mood to do it. If we desire to be like Christ, we must make forgiveness a part of our nature. If we desire to create an environment of forgiveness, we must live like Christ.

When Conflict Occurs

While working on this book, Carol McGinnis and I had two major disagreements. Some people found this amusing, and later so did we. After all, we were working on a book about forgiveness. Didn't that mean we should always agree?

Not necessarily.

Choosing forgiveness as our goal and adopting attitudes that will promote forgiveness will not always prevent conflict. Some conflict is inevitable because we're all imperfect. We all sin; we fail; we make mistakes. We have different perspectives, different expectations, and the result is conflict. Conflict is not wrong, but our reactions to it may be.

We don't need to be afraid of conflict. Ignoring it can only multiply the underlying problems, erect barriers, and interfere with our growth and intimacy. Many Christians shy away from facing differences. Some actually think it's not spiritual to disagree. Francis A. Schaeffer tells us, "We have a greater possibility of showing what Jesus is speaking about here in the midst of our differences, than we do if we are not differing" *(The Mark of the Christian,* InterVarsity Press, p. 31). A sign of spiritual maturity is not avoiding conflict, but being able to face it without losing our self-control.

Since many of our problems come about because of our inability to communicate effectively, it is important for us to work on this skill. Gary Collins offers several helpful hints on communication in his book *Calm Down.*

"Communication involves a sincere desire to understand and to be understood," Collins says. To do this we need to listen carefully, concentrate on getting and stating facts, and avoid the use of emotionally explosive phrases such as, "You never" or "You always." Ridiculing, name calling, interrupting, sarcasm, criticism, or "put downs" aren't helpful either. We need to say what we really think and mean. "Communication requires flexibility and willingness to overlook personality quirks," he adds. "That takes determination and maturity, but then so does good communication" (Christian Herald Books, pp. 51-55).

Many times the cause of our conflict lies deeper than the problem we're discussing at the moment. In a sense, we're attacking the wrong problem. Explains Creath Davis, founder and director of the Christian Concern Foundation in Dallas, Texas:

> Attacking the wrong problem never resolves the real one. Each one of us has a list of emotionally safe, acceptable problems and of dangerous, unacceptable ones. Every time one of these dangerous, unacceptable problems begins to appear we will be tempted to substitute a more acceptable one with which to struggle. The majority of the people who have come to me for counseling have presented a problem to be resolved which was not the problem at all (*How to Win in a Crisis,* Zondervan, pp. 24-25).

We won't solve our problems if we won't admit they exist. We also won't solve our problems if we view conflicts as personal attacks.

"People with weak self-esteem must win an argument at all costs. To lose signifies a loss of identity," writes Cecil G. Osborne (*The Art of Getting Along with People,* Zondervan, p. 48). If we find ourselves desiring to win at all costs, we would be wise to ask ourselves *Why?* If it's because we feel our self-worth is being questioned, we need to take care of that problem on our knees before our Father in prayer. In some cases, professional counseling may be required.

Our conflicts can give us clues to other areas where we need to improve, because God gives us "just the right parents, mates, children, and associates to develop the Christian graces in our lives" (Matilda Nordtvedt, *Defeating Despair and Depression,* Moody Press, p. 33). When we disagree, we should take a long look at ourselves before assigning blame to the other person.

It's important for us to recognize the authority of Scripture. The Bible has the solution to many of our conflicts, if only we'll pay attention to it. "All Scripture is God-breathed and is useful for teaching, rebuking, correcting and training in righteousness" (2 Tim. 3:16).

Prayer is another spiritual resource useful in resolving conflicts. Prayer is most helpful when we are completely honest with God. We must ask for God's help to see our weaknesses and strengths, and for the love, courage, and wisdom to reconcile.

Above all, we should allow love to guide us to a solution. Love knows how to look after our own interests as well as the interests of others (Phil. 2:4-11). Love knows when we should lay aside our rights (Rom. 12:10; Phil. 2:3; Matt. 5:40-42). Love knows when it is best to submit and to serve others (Eph. 5:21; Mark 10:43-45; John 13:14). Love is the key to resolving our conflicts and to living in forgiveness.

Forgiveness Is Important

Without forgiveness, our friendships will not last, or they will not develop beyond a superficial level. When we are forgiving, we allow our friends to be themselves; we give them "the security of knowing they can blow it and still be loved and totally forgiven with nothing held over their heads" (Jerry Cook with Stanley C. Baldwin, *Love, Acceptance and Forgiveness,* Regal Books, p. 90).

In marriage, forgiveness is the lubrication for friction. The divorce rate is soaring today. Many reasons are often cited, such as lack of communication, lack of commitment, immaturity, differing goals. But another reason is a lack of forgiveness. Billy Graham once said that a successful marriage requires *two* very good forgivers. Others have called forgiveness one of the pillars supporting marriage, one of the ways to make marriage divorce-proof, and the way to sustain true marriage.

In the home, forgiveness is important because it helps shape a child's character. If a child sees forgiveness practiced, he will learn how to forgive. If he does not see forgiveness, chances are he will have difficulty extending forgiveness to others.

In the church, forgiveness is one of the characteristics that identifies us as Christ's followers. "All men will know that you are My disciples if you love one another," Christ promised (John 13:35).

> Christ's unique plan was that non-Christians come to know of His love through Christians in proper relationship with one another. Though Christ would no longer be physically present, people could learn of His love through His followers who would continue to love one another as He had loved them while He was on the earth (Gene Getz, *Loving One Another,* Victor Books, p. 30).

Unfortunately, many Christians are unforgiving and lack love. This discredits the Gospel and drives people away. I wonder if this is one reason for the popularity of cults. Many ex-cultists claim they were originally attracted to the cult by the kindness, acceptance, and love they received from its members. We should keep this in mind since we are often so empty in these areas.

Larry Christenson writes that the greatest power Jesus left His church is forgiveness.

> Where the church has practiced this lesson, she has been unconquerable. Where she has failed to practice it, she has been divided and defeated, a spectacle of shame before men and angels. . . . Where the church has practiced unilateral forgiveness among its membership, and toward those who might persecute her from the outside, she has been unconquerable. . . . The world can never break the church.

The power of hell cannot break the church. The only thing that can break the church is her own unwillingness to live in forgiveness *(The Renewed Mind,* Bethany Fellowship, pp. 54-57).

The Other Side of Forgiveness

So far we've been discussing our responsibility to be forgiving. But what should we do when we offend others? We're not perfect, so it's bound to happen. What should we do then?

11
The Other Side of Forgiveness

> The son said to him, "Father, I have sinned against heaven and against you. I am no longer worthy to be called your son" (Luke 15:21).

The spring was unusually warm. King David was having problems sleeping, so he got up from his bed to walk around on the palace roof. As he gazed across Jerusalem, he saw a beautiful woman bathing in the open inner courtyard of a nearby house. He was attracted to her and sent a man to find our her name.

"Isn't this Bathsheba, the daughter of Eliam and wife of Uriah the Hittite?" the man asked.

David sent messengers to bring Bathsheba to him. She was escorted to the palace where she spent the night.

Several weeks later King David received a simple message from Bathsheba. "I am pregnant."

David immediately began to plan a cover-up. He sent word to Joab, the captain of his army, asking that Bathsheba's husband be sent home from the battle.

When Uriah arrived in Jerusalem, David asked for a progress report on the war and then gave Uriah permission to spend a night at home before returning to battle. But Uriah didn't. He slept with the servants at the entrance to the palace. The next day when David asked him why, Uriah said, "The ark and Israel and Judah are staying in tents, and my master Joab and my lord's men are camped in the open fields. How could I go to my house to eat and drink and lie with my wife? As surely as you live, I will not do such a thing!"

David became uneasy. He asked Uriah to stay another day in Jerusalem. That evening David invited Uriah to the palace for a meal and made Uriah drunk. David had hoped this would make Uriah forget his principles and go to his wife. But he didn't. Once again, he spent the night with the servants.

Desperate now, David changed his tactic. The next morning he sent Uriah back to battle with a sealed letter to Joab. The letter ordered Joab to put Uriah in the front line of battle where the fighting was fiercest.

Joab did as he was commanded and Uriah was killed. After Bathsheba's time of mourning was complete, David brought her into his house and she became one of his wives. David was guilty of adultery and plotting murder, yet he was called a man after God's own heart. How can that be? (See 2 Sam. 11; 1 Sam. 13:14). Luke wrote, "After removing Saul, [God] made David their king. He testified concerning him: 'I have found David son of Jesse a man after My own heart; he will do everything I want him to do'" (Acts 13:22).

The Secret of Spiritual Health

When the Prophet Nathan confronted David with his sin, David had several choices. He could have tried to deny it, or justify it, or rationalize it. Instead, he simply admitted it. "I have sinned against the Lord," he said. (See 2 Sam. 12.) His full confession to God is recorded in Psalm 51.

Throughout his life whenever David was confronted with his sin, he sincerely admitted his wrong and turned back to God to ask for mercy. This was the secret of David's spiritual strength. This can also be the source of our spiritual strength.

When We Sin

When we receive Jesus Christ as our personal Saviour, all of our sins—past, present, and future—are forgiven. God no longer condemns us; our legal standing before Him is, "Not guilty!" (Rom. 8:1) But let's not get the idea it really doesn't matter how we live. Sin still has consequences.

As Christians, when we sin we are not jeopardizing our membership in God's family, but we are jeopardizing our fellowship with Him. Our relationship with God depends on our spiritual birth, but our fellowship depends on our obedience. The Parable of the Prodigal Son illustrates this principle. When the son left his father, legally he was still his father's son, but their fellowship was broken. Their fellowship was restored when the son confessed his sin. Since sin disrupts our fellowship with God, which results in a lack of spiritual growth and ineffective prayer life, we must confess our failures to Him. Confessing to Him often opens the door for us to more easily ask others to forgive us.

Guilt: A Red Light

King David did not confess his sin right away. It wasn't until after his child was born that Nathan confronted David (2 Sam. 11:27—12:1). During those months David suffered from unrelenting guilt. "When I kept silent, my bones wasted away through my groaning all day long. For day and night Your hand was heavy upon me; my strength was sapped as in the heat of the summer. Then I acknowledged my sin to You and did not cover up my iniquity. I said, 'I will confess my transgressions to the Lord'—and You forgave the guilt of my sin" (Ps. 32:3-5).

Guilt is like a red traffic light. It's a signal telling us to stop, examine our lives, and see if there is anything we must confess. Most of us know what guilt feels like, but many of us don't realize that there are two types of guilt: true and false.

True guilt is our inborn, God-given response to our violations of God's laws. But because our consciences are molded by a flawed society and imperfect people, our consciences are not always accurate and we can suffer from false guilt. False guilt is "feeling guilty for something that in reality does not violate any of the laws of God" (Frank B. Minirth and Paul Meier, *Happiness Is a Choice,* Baker Book House, p. 69). False guilt is usually very hard to pin down and arises in response to thoughts, feelings, or temptations, rather than a specific action. Or it arises from participating in an activity that is not specifically forbidden in Scripture, yet is considered sinful by some people. It also can arise from something that happened long ago. The cure for false guilt is not seeking forgiveness, but asking God to help us leave those feelings behind and get on with life (Philip Yancey and Tim Stafford, *Unhappy Secrets of the Christian Life,* Zondervan, pp. 51-53). However, we can only get rid of our true guilt by seeking forgiveness from God, and when appropriate, from the person we wronged.

To determine whether our guilt is true or false we should: check out what the Bible has to say; talk the matter over with God; or ask a spiritually mature person for advice. If we determine that we are suffering from true guilt, we must confess the wrong.

What Is Confession?
Confession simply means admitting a sin or fault. It is a description of what happened. That may sound simple, but confession is difficult. It takes courage, humility, and honesty.

First, our pride is at stake. We rationalize, "How can a nice person like me do something to require forgiveness?" It can be humiliating to say, "I was wrong and I am sorry. Please forgive me." Stubbornness enters in too. Pride says, "I can't be wrong," but stubbornness says, "I know I'm wrong, but I will not ask to be forgiven."

Bill Gothard lists some of the most common excuses we use for not confessing and asking forgiveness:

"It happened a long time ago."

"It was such a small offense."

"The one I wronged has moved away."
"Things have gotten better."
"I'm just being too sensitive."
"No one's perfect."
"They won't understand."
"Making it right will involve money which I don't have."
"I'll do it later."
"The other person was mostly wrong."
"If I purpose not to do it again, won't that be enough?"
"They're not Christians—what will they think?"
("Clear Conscience," *Institute in Basic Youth Conflicts*, pp. 15-18).

Why We Must Confess

It is through confession that we find God's mercy. "He who conceals his sins does not prosper, but whoever confesses and renounces them finds mercy" (Prov. 28:13).

Without confessing our wrongs and making things right between ourselves and others, our worship is unacceptable to God. Jesus said, "If you are offering your gift at the altar and there remember that your brother has something against you, leave your gift there in front of the altar. First go and be reconciled to your brother; then come and offer your gift" (Matt. 5:23-24).

One by-product of confession is a clear conscience which is essential to having an adequate self-acceptance (Tim LaHaye, *How to Win Over Depression,* Zondervan, p. 157). Our joy and freedom are restored as we confess our wrongs. If we confess, it'll make it easier for others to admit their wrongs.

Since there is a connection between some illnesses and guilt, confession can heal us. James advises us to confess to one another so that we may be healed (James 5:16).

Confession to our fellow Christians makes our love visible to the world. "If I am not willing to say, 'I'm sorry,' when I have wronged somebody else—especially when I have not loved him—I have not even started to think about the meaning of a Christian oneness which the world can see. The world has a right to question whether I am a Christian" (Francis A. Schaeffer, *The Mark of the Christian,* InterVarsity Press, p. 22).

Confession is a sign of spiritual and emotional maturity. Eighteenth century English poet and critic Alexander Pope once said, "A man should never be ashamed to own he has been wrong, which is but saying, in other words, that he is wiser today than he was yesterday."

Confession does not necessarily remove the consequences of sin. For example, when David confessed, his infant son did not return to life. But God can use even the consequences of our sin to teach us lessons and conform us to His Son's image.

Three Types of Confession

We must confess to God all sins. But only those against a particular individual should be confessed to the individual, and only those against a group or congregation should be confessed publicly. A rule to follow here is this: confession should only be as public as the knowledge of the act.

First, let's take a look at confession to God. Confession begins with being honest with ourselves. "We cannot confess to God that which we will not admit to ourselves" (Cecil Osborne, *Release From Fear and Anxiety,* Word Books, p. 98).

Confession means agreeing with God that this action is indeed wrong. Confession does not try to justify or explain the matter. Confession is not ignoring or dodging our sin or trying to work the matter out for ourselves.

True confession is specific, not general. For example: "Lord, I hate _____, and because of this hate, I attempted to destroy his reputation today by _____," instead of, "Lord, I hate people."

Confession does not beg or plead for forgiveness. "If we confess our sins, He is faithful and just and will forgive us our sins and purify us from all unrighteousness" (1 John 1:9).

We can confess an unlimited number of times and at any time. Our confession should be directed to Jesus Christ, our Mediator. "For there is one God and one Mediator between God and men, the man Christ Jesus" (1 Tim. 2:5).

Confession to Others

First we must determine what we need to confess to others. We should ask God to activate our memories. The attitudes of others toward us can also give us clues to the things for which we should ask forgiveness. It might be a good idea to get into the habit of taking a few minutes each evening to review the day's events to see if we have offended anyone.

Though it is important to ask forgiveness for specific acts, it may be even more important to seek forgiveness for the attitudes underlying the offenses. Says Bill Gothard, "It is important to distinguish between immediate offenses and basic offenses. They are not always the same. It does little good to ask forgiveness for a small offense when in reality that offense is only a fractional part of a much greater offense" *(Basic Youth Conflicts,* p. 6). The basic attitudes which give birth to our specific actions include ungratefulness, stubbornness, untruthfulness, indifference, bitterness, laziness, rudeness, thoughtlessness, and resentment. We can offend by being judgmental, unaccepting, inconsiderate, harsh, flippant, and critical. We can offend by misinterpreting actions, forming opinions, ignoring someone, or carrying a chip on our shoulders.

We should compile a list of people from whom we must ask forgiveness. Then we should seek out those persons in private.

If someone is unavailable for a personal meeting, a phone call or letter may work. But we must recognize the limitations of these means.

When we meet with someone to confess our wrongs, we shouldn't try to justify ourselves or shift the blame. We should specifically ask for forgiveness and wait for a response. Saying,

"I'm sorry," is not the same as asking, "Will you forgive me?" When we only say we're sorry, we're admitting that a wrong has been done—but we aren't taking responsibility for it. Accepting the blame is essential. Say, "God has shown me I was wrong to _____, and I've come to ask your forgiveness."

We should be careful to speak the truth in love in order to cause as little suffering as possible. Some things may be better left unsaid (Eph. 4:15; 5:1-2).

Since it is impossible for others to see into our hearts and know our intentions, we should show signs of our repentance (Matt. 3:8; Acts 26:20). We should make restitution if that is possible. For example, stolen money can be returned; damaged property can be repaired.

What If . . . .

When we go to someone to ask forgiveness, there's always a chance that the person won't forgive us. What can we do if this happens?

Proverbs 16:7 promises, "When a man's ways are pleasing to the Lord, he makes even his enemies live at peace with him." But, claims Charles Swindoll, since the word *immediate* doesn't appear in this verse, it may be awhile before we are at peace with our "enemy" ("Forgiving Like a Servant Forgives," from an *Insight for Living* tape). If someone refuses to forgive us after we have sincerely sought forgiveness, we have fulfilled our obligation. We cannot change others and we are not responsible for someone else's actions. We can only wait.

In some cases, asking for forgiveness may make the situation worse. On one hand, Bill Gothard explains, the offended has been blaming you for his angry feelings. But on the other hand, this person may have been feeling guilty for his attitude. When we ask for forgiveness, we upset this balance of blame and guilt. "When there is no blame to justify and balance his past wrongs, his guilt intensifies" *(Basic Youth Conflicts,* p. 33).

If we can't locate the ones we've offended, we can ask God to help us find them. If He wants us to find the people we've offended He's more than capable of helping us do it. Actually, He's probably more interested in us making things right than we are.

Benefits of Asking Forgiveness

I have been corresponding with a number of prison inmates who are Christians. Many of them face rejection by loved ones whom they caused to suffer. One young prisoner said his parents asked him not to come home at the time he was paroled. He was no longer welcome there. This hurt him deeply. Most of these young men would give most anything, they have said, to receive forgiveness from those they have hurt. They have received God's forgiveness, but people have difficulty giving theirs.

I have suggested to two of these young men that they specifically ask forgiveness for having hurt their loved ones so deeply. Just recently, the one who wasn't welcome at home told me his parents have forgiven him. I am thrilled over this. However, the inmate isn't sure his mother fully understands about his faith in Christ and what forgiveness really means. The results, of course, lie in God's hands. But my young prisoner friend did ask his parents to forgive him for humiliating and hurting them so much. That was a gigantic step in the right direction.

It is so hard to say, "I need your forgiveness. I love you. I want to be rid of the guilt of hurting you purposely or accidentally. Will you forgive me?" But if we can do this, we will be 100 percent happier, our joy will run deeper, and we will clear away much of the smog that has enveloped our lives. Barriers will break as we reach through all the misunderstandings and unjust hurts and show Christ's love.

My husband's brother and his wife, Byron and Esther, had lived apart from the rest of the family for years. We met them briefly on rare occasions. I always believed I liked them, but I certainly did not know them. We had prayed for them, knowing they did not know Jesus Christ in a personal way. But that is as far as we ventured in our responsibility. They lived out of the state and we were seldom in touch.

One day word came from them that they wanted to spend Thanksgiving weekend with us. We were delighted. When they arrived late one evening after driving for hours, we greeted them warmly and attempted to make them comfortable. We brought out the hot coffee and cookies and proceeded to talk.

Bob and I were curious about what *really* brought them our way. They told us many things about their lives that were most revealing. But the most thrilling of all was that they had both recently received Jesus Christ as their Saviour and Lord.

Finally Byron stood and placed his hand on Bob's shoulder and said, to our astonishment, "We have hated you for years. We really don't know why, but we have come here to your home to face you and ask, Will you forgive us please? God has placed a warm love in our hearts for you now, and we want you to know this. It has been so important to us that we felt we must meet face to face."

Our arms went around one another, and we wept and rejoiced as we forgave them. After that weekend they went to visit Mother, for Byron also asked for her forgiveness for having hated her so many years. I can only imagine that joyful reunion. Before he left, he told us quietly, "I can't ask Dad to forgive me for hating him for his rejection of me as a kid, because he is dead. But I am going to his grave, and kneel there and ask God to forgive me for hating my father."

God gave them the courage to follow through on this venture for Him. We respected them for what God was helping them to do.

Asking forgiveness can clear our consciences before God and man. A young college girl from Florida new in her faith in Jesus Christ was an unhappy Christian. In talking extensively with a Christian counselor, some facts from her past were uncovered. As a child, she had been repeatedly molested by her own father and she hated him bitterly. She was depressed and deeply disturbed.

The counselor asked if she had ever considered asking her father to forgive her.

"Ask *him* to forgive *me?*"she exploded. "For what? He is the one who has wrecked my life! Why doesn't he ask me to forgive him?"

"If he would ask you, could you do it?" the counselor asked.

They were both thoughtful and quiet for a moment. Then the counselor cautiously said, "But you hate him. You could ask forgiveness for that. The Bible says anyone who hates his brother is the same as a murderer."

After thinking and praying that through, the young girl visited her dad, and asked him to forgive her for hating him all those many years.

Her father broke down weeping. "My dear girl, I have waited and longed for this day," he said. "I have lived with unforgiven guilt for so long."

They forgave each other and had a wonderful reunion. The daughter shared her new faith in Christ with her father. The Holy Spirit had prepared his heart and he opened his heart and life to the Lord. He received Christ as his Saviour that day.

Several weeks later, the man suddenly died. It was a shock, yet his daughter had a clear conscience. She was glad she had made things right with him and that he had made things right with God.

Asking for forgiveness is a way to make our faith in Christ visible to an unbelieving world. Bob and I have some dear friends, Elizabeth and Bill, whose 12-year-old daughter died unexpectedly. She had been ill only a few days with flu-like symptoms. Suddenly, her illness became desperately serious. Because their own physician was on vacation, they hurried Nancy to the nearest doctor.

By then she was in a coma. Bill dashed into the doctor's office and shouted, "My daughter is in a coma and too ill to bring inside. I think she's dying!" He insisted that the doctor go to the car with him.

But the doctor refused to see Nancy. Office hours were over

and he was going home.

Bill exploded. I don't know all he said to that doctor, but it was anything but Christlike. He rushed back into his car, and in a panic, raced to the hospital emergency entrance. Nancy received immediate attention, but by morning she had died. It had all happened so suddenly. It was indeed a shock. We, along with countless others, were saddened and went to comfort Bill and Elizabeth as best we could.

However, Bill could not be at peace with himself. He knew his outburst at the doctor's office was far from Christ-honoring. He explained that his two natures churned within him. One said he was right; the other told him he was wrong.

The doctor is the one who was wrong, Bill reasoned. *He didn't have to be rude and uncaring. It was such a small favor I had asked him, really. It would have taken only a few more minutes of his precious time. He refused to show any compassion. Perhaps Nancy would still be living had he taken a moment to look at her. I certainly reacted in a normal way under the circumstances.*

Bill continued to allow his anger to lash out, but he was only harming himself. "I had struck a gong intended for someone else," Bill said, "but the reverberations kept pounding back at me. I knew it was impossible to unring a bell, but it would be less bruising if I grabbed the clapper so that the clanging of hate inside me would cease. This bitter and blaming attitude, gnawing and corroding my fellowship with Christ, had to be dealt with."

Even before the funeral, Bill returned to that doctor's office. In the presence of the doctor, the nurse and the secretary who had heard his outburst, he told them Nancy had died. Complete and solemn silence followed that statement. Then, quietly, Bill told them he was a Christian and had no right to act as he had in their office. He said he wanted his life to please Christ, and he knew he had let his Lord down. The Lord had forgiven him, and in the face of his heart anguish and deep grief, Bill asked the doctor to forgive him for his unchristian behavior. He also tried to free the doctor of any sense of guilt regarding Nancy's death.

I don't know how this affected the doctor. I would assume he was literally astounded. Bill sensed immediate release from the emotions which had bound him.

"It was like my spirit had taken a warm shower in God's love," he explains. "And my heart seemed to hear Nancy say, 'Good! Your bitterness could not have brought me back.' And only then was I able to release Nancy calmly and with confidence into God's eternal care.

"Oh, if we could all just learn we don't need to be in control—we only need to be the house for the Holy Spirit. Then we can allow God to be who He is—the Blessed Controller of all things."

12

God Is in Control

So then, those who suffer according to God's will should commit themselves to their faithful Creator and continue to do good (1 Peter 4:19).

A dam broke in the north Georgia city of Toccoa on November 6, 1977. Flood waters swept through the campus of Toccoa Falls College, an interdenominational Bible college, at an estimated 50 to 150 miles per hour. Thirty-nine people were killed. What about the survivors?

Many said the experience made their faith stronger. Some were joyful; some said they felt honored to have gone through the flood. Most claimed they were peaceful and hadn't asked the inevitable question, "Why?" Their secret? Faith in a sovereign all-powerful God (K. Neill Foster with Eric Mills, *Dam Break in Georgia,* Horizon House).

Our Sovereign God

The Bible tells us that God is sovereign:

Acknowledge and take to heart this day that the Lord is God in heaven above and on the earth below. There is no other (Deut. 4:39).

155

Let them know that You, whose name is the Lord—
that You alone are the Most High over all the earth
(Ps. 83:18).

There is no God apart from Me, a righteous God and
a Saviour; there is none but Me (Isa. 45:21).

"Do You refuse to speak to me?" Pilate said. "Don't
You realize I have power either to free You or to
crucify You?"

Jesus answered, "You would have no power over
me if it were not given to you from above" (John
19:10-11).

But What of Suffering?

One sunny afternoon I was relaxing in the hammock underneath an oak tree. Gazing up through the maze of leafy
branches, I noticed the many peculiar twists and turns of some
branches. Some were misshapen and distorted; others carried
knots, humps, and scars. There were thin and scraggly
branches and strong and stout branches. Yet, with all its
deformities, the tree was beautiful. I wondered how many years
of severe weather and storms it had withstood. How many
violent and uncontrollable winds and other elements of nature
had helped shape that tree?

That tree didn't just happen. It has withstood bending,
twisting, turning, and growing under conditions that were
often adverse. But had it not been for those adversities, that
oak tree wouldn't be half as strong as it is.

This same principle holds true in the spiritual realm. What
seem to be buffetings and setbacks apparently are all a part of
God's great plan for our maturity and development. Inner
beauty and strength are developed from adversity. Peter
writes, "Now for a little while you may have had to suffer grief
in all kinds of trials. These have come so that your faith—of
greater worth than gold, which perishes even though refined by

fire—may be proved genuine and may result in praise, glory, and honor when Jesus Christ is revealed (1 Peter 1:6-7).

Why do problems and adversities come our way? To prove or authenticate our faith. Scripture also suggests other reasons for our problems:

- We live in a fallen world (Gen. 3; John 16:33).
- We live in an unpredictable world (Ecc. 9:11).
- Sin has consequences (Gal. 6:7-8).
- Satan is active in human affairs and attempts to destroy our faith (see the Book of Job; 2 Cor. 4:4).
- God disciplines His children (Heb. 12:7-11).
- Suffering is a normal part of the Christian life (1 Peter 2:19-21; Rom. 8:17; Matt. 10:38; 2 Tim. 3:12; Phil. 1:29).
- Problems teach us to rely on God (2 Cor. 1:8-9).

Despite these hints, many times we don't know the specific reasons behind our problems. But we do not need to know the "why" to cope—we just need to know God.

If anyone ever had reason to be hostile and question God's control, it was the Apostle Paul. He once cataloged his sufferings:

I have worked much harder, been in prison more frequently, been flogged more severely, and been exposed to death again and again. Five times I received from the Jews the forty lashes minus one. Three times I was beaten with rods, once I was stoned, three times I was shipwrecked, I spent a night and a day in the open sea, I have been constantly on the move. I have been in danger from rivers, in danger from bandits, in danger from my own countrymen, in danger from Gentiles; in danger in the city, in danger in the country, in danger at sea; and in danger from false brothers. I have labored and toiled and have often gone without sleep; I have known hunger and thirst and have often gone without food; I have been cold and naked. Besides everything else, I face daily the pressure of my concern for all the churches (2 Cor. 11:23-28).

This adversity did not dismay Paul. He told Timothy that he was not ashamed of his sufferings "because I know whom I have believed" (2 Tim. 1:12).

Knowing our Lord is the key because our viewpoints are narrow and our understanding is limited. (See Isa. 55:8-9.)

Our Promise

God can take everything that touches us, both the good and the bad, and use it to reach His number one goal for us: to make us like His dear Son, Jesus Christ. "And we know that in all things God works for the good of those who love Him, who have been called according to His purpose. For those God foreknew He also predestined to be conformed to the likeness of His Son, that He might be the firstborn among many brothers" (Rom. 8:28-29; see also Gal. 4:19; 2 Cor. 3:18).

The pattern God is weaving in our lives looks beautiful from heaven's side; but from our perspective, we only see the tangles, knots, and mistakes. Each event in our lives is a piece of a puzzle. When all the pieces are fitted together, we have a beautiful picture.

God uses a variety of instruments, including our offenders, to conform us to the image of His Son. When faced with an offense, if we do not react properly to it we destroy its possible benefit. But as we learn to respond properly, we become more like Jesus Christ.

Our Response

Since God is in control, nothing can enter our lives that we can't forgive—because God uses everything to make us like Christ. I'm not saying God is directly responsible for the bad things in our lives, because He is not the author of evil or confusion. But He is powerful enough to take those bad things and use them for our ultimate good (1 Cor. 14:33; James 1:13).

Peter wrote, "So then, those who suffer according to God's

will should commit themselves to their faithful Creator and continue to do good" (1 Peter 4:19).

Bringing the Good Out of the Bad

After Beverly Benton was assaulted, she and her husband Larry could have reacted with anger, resentment, and bitterness. But through the power of the Holy Spirit, they were able to forgive Beverly's assailant. They contacted the man once he was apprehended to express their forgiveness. That experience made them realize the need for the preaching of the Gospel among inmates. The result? The couple began P.S. (Personal Saviour) Ministries, a division of Campus Crusade for Christ International. Now their goal is to place trained "para-chaplain" or "associate-chaplain" staff members in every federal and state penal institution in North America.

* * *

Charles Swindoll tells the story of a seminary student who had prayed for a "significant ministry" during his summer vacation. He was hoping for a position with a church or some Christian organization. But summer came and no position had opened up. Summer was slipping away, and the student needed a job, so he took the only one available—driving a bus on Chicago's south side.

He hadn't been on the job many days when a gang of youths assaulted him. The student decided to press charges. Police rounded up the gang and a hearing was scheduled. As the student sat in the courtroom looking at his assailants, his bitterness was replaced with compassion.

The student requested permission to speak. He astounded everyone by asking the judge to tally the days of punishment against the youths and allow him to serve the time in jail in their place.

Then the student turned to the gang and said quietly, "It's because I forgive you."

The judge told the young man he was out of order and that such a thing had never been done before. But the young man disagreed and spent the next few minutes explaining how Jesus Christ had died on the cross in our place.

The young man was denied his request. But later as he visited the youths in jail, he led most of them to faith in Jesus Christ. That was the beginning of his "significant ministry" to many others on the south side of Chicago (Charles R. Swindoll, Insight for Living tape, "Forgiving Like a Servant Forgives").

* * *

Joseph was sold into slavery by his jealous brothers for 20 shekels of silver. Several years later, after the Egyptian Pharaoh had put Joseph in charge of all the land, Joseph had an opportunity to take revenge.

A severe famine had struck the land and because God had revealed to Joseph there would be a famine, Egypt had prepared for it. Egypt was the only nation around with excess grain. When Joseph's brothers came to Egypt to buy grain, Joseph could have refused. He could have had them jailed. Instead, he said:

> Do not be distressed and do not be angry with yourselves for selling me here, because it was to save lives that God sent me ahead of you. For two years now there has been famine in the land, and for the next five years there will not be plowing and reaping. But God sent me ahead of you to preserve for you a remnant on earth and to save your lives by a great deliverance. So then, it was not you who sent me here, but God (Gen. 45:5-8).

Later, after Joseph's father died, Joseph again assured his brothers he would not take revenge. Joseph believed God had been in control even as he was sold into slavery. "You intended to harm me," he said, "but God intended it for good to accomplish what is now being done, the saving of many lives"

(50:20; see also chaps. 37—50).

*   *   *

Some have asked, "How could anything good come out of something as horrible as the rape and murder of your daughter?"

I have learned to see God's hand at work through Diane's death. He has used Tom as an instrument to help shave off some rough edges in my life, to cut back apathy and lack of compassion, and to help remove selfishness and thoughtless desires. I know all the deep suffering and anguish my family and I have endured has helped us grow spiritually. We turn our pain and sorrow over to God for His use. In so doing, He stretched our hearts and minds till they hurt. Yet He also filled us with His overflowing love. We praise and thank Him for His plans and for the grace He gave us to allow Him to work in our lives.

It appears one of His purposes has been to allow us to share with others the importance of forgiveness. God continues to teach us how very important this subject is. We do not share scriptural forgiveness because we have it mastered; no, far from it. We share it because God is constantly teaching us its worth.

God has allowed me to do this in many ways. Besides speaking for women's fellowships, retreats, seminars, and Christian Women's Clubs, God has brought my husband and me in contact with a number of Christian prison inmates who had read a magazine article I had written on forgiveness. We have had an ongoing ministry of this kind for some time now.

Unfortunately, prisoners are often the last to receive any kind of Christian forgiveness. So many of them are lonely. One 19-year-old told us that we were the *first* ones who had ever visited him. His eyes misted as he said that, and so did mine.

Another young man told us his parents never wanted him to return home; they had been too hurt and humiliated by him.

He understands this and doesn't blame them, but it still hurts because he loves his family.

Each one of these men is some mother's son, and we are learning just how much the moms and dads hurt too. As parents, none of us know how our children will turn out. Some sons and daughters who have had the best homes and upbringing are in prison serving time. Others are breaking their parents' hearts outside of prison.

When we visited with Tom, we learned then just how deeply hurt his own parents were and are. This was perhaps our first bit of insight into the hearts of the moms and dads whose children are in prison. Those parents now have our prayers.

When my husband retired in May of 1981, we began to pray for God's leading for our lives in retirement. God has seen fit to bring these special ministries right to our doorstep. We thank Him that He is allowing us to share His love and forgiveness with prisoners in this way.

I often wonder how many people, in prison or not, would be far more happy and free if only we, as Christians, would extend genuine forgiveness to them? I am often haunted by what I read in one of Charles Watson's newsletters: "God had totally forgiven me for my ugly crimes, but my Christian brothers and sisters can't." I would say it a little differently: "My Christian brothers and sisters *won't!*" That is what it boils down to. It isn't a matter of *"Can* I forgive?" but *"Will* I?"

Epilogue

A great number of people have discussed their thoughts and questions with me regarding what God has been accomplishing in our lives these past few years. Many rejoice with us and some are skeptical. I think I can understand this, and I would like to take the opportunity now to answer some of the most common questions.

Q: *When Diane died tragically, and some would say prematurely, did you ask the inevitable question: "Why, Lord?"*

A: I can honestly say I did not, but my husband did. He said he would have gladly died in her place for Diane had only begun to really live, and his earthly life, at best, was more than half over. Diane's death was completely unexpected and a shock and our reaction was human: we wept, we anguished in our spirits, but I personally did not question God's wisdom.

God doesn't make mistakes: He always has everything in His divine control (Eph. 1:11). These biblical truths were instilled in me as a small child, and I believe they helped bring me to the place where I trusted God with Diane's death despite the agonizing pain.

Long before we knew who Diane's attacker was, God had performed His miraculous work of forgiveness in our hearts. The forgiving, as far as I was concerned, had been done. It would not have made any difference who the person was—his age, his race, his background, whether or not he was "sick," on drugs or alcohol, or destitute. We knew this person needed Jesus Christ as His Saviour and he needed forgiveness for his horrible crime.

On other occasions, I *have* questioned God. Nevertheless, I always seem to be brought back to the basic fact of God's loving purpose for each one of us. The psalmist tells us our times are in His hands (Ps. 31:15), and when He is finished with us here, He takes us home. This, of course, did not prevent me from hurting deeply. Separation of any kind is a hurting experience.

> *Q: Didn't you have Diane covered with the blood of Christ? Wouldn't it have been impossible for her attacker to have harmed her if this were true?*

A: Frankly, I wasn't prepared for this question when I first heard it, and I couldn't answer it to my satisfaction on the spot. Now I think I can. I assume this statement stems from the account found in the Book of Exodus. Chapters 11 and 12 tell us the Children of Israel's redemption from the plague on the firstborn required that the blood of the paschal lamb be sprinkled on the doorpost of each home to guarantee the occupants' physical safety. It is also true our redemption from sin and its curse on the human race required the blood of Christ, God's lamb. Just as Israel received physical protection by the blood of a slain lamb, so we receive eternal protection by the blood of God's Son.

Scripture teaches that God is forever watching over us, that He does not slumber nor sleep (Ps. 121:3-4). "The eyes of the Lord are on the righteous and His ears are attentive to their cry" (34:15). David assures us that we cannot flee God's presence, that He has hemmed us in "behind and before," and that His hand is laid upon us (139:5). "The eyes of the Lord are on those who fear Him, on those whose hope is in His unfailing love" (33:18). There is no question that the Lord is ever watching, caring for, and protecting us.

However, I do not find in any of these verses an indication that this physical protection is provided by the blood of Christ. I can find plenty of evidence that the blood of the Lamb of God protects us from eternal death. John the Baptist proclaimed, "Look, the Lamb of God, who takes away the sin of the world" (John 1:29). In Hebrews 9:22 we read, "Without the shedding of blood there is no forgiveness." "Blessed is he whose transgressions are forgiven, whose sins are covered" (Ps. 32:1).

If we, as believers, can claim physical protection through the blood of Christ, why were His disciples in the early church persecuted, tortured, and martyred for their faith? Many times God *did* give physical protection. There are several examples of this in Paul's life: when he was stoned and left for dead (Acts 14:19); when he was shipwrecked (Acts 27; 2 Cor. 11:25); when he handled the poisonous snake (Acts 28:1-6). Paul was chained in prison even though he was innocent, and later was martyred for his faith in Jesus Christ. There are many such examples in the New Testament and among first-century Christians.

Our eternal security does not guarantee our physical safety. If we would claim another's or our own physical protection through Christ's blood, there would be no disasters or tragedies. But life is not this way.

I had committed Diane to God and I knew she belonged to Him. He would take care of her in His own best way. I could not claim physical protection for her any more than I could claim someone's eternal salvation for them. I was in constant prayer for God's hand upon Diane's life, and I believe it was there.

Q: *If you have forgiven your daughter's killer, why aren't you campaigning for his parole? Don't the two go together if you have truly forgiven?*

A: Our forgiveness was a personal act. It is not connected with what the law has done or may do. We do not have the authority to be involved in the legal aspects of forgiving Tom's crime. We believe any criminal should pay the price for his crime. This is scriptural.

Therefore, we have not felt led to campaign for his parole. The decision to parole him would be up to the State. But this does not hinder us from extending personal forgiveness for his crime. Our attitudes regarding our role in Tom's parole could change if he became a sincere believer in Christ and showed true repentance.

I have forgiven my daughter's killer in the *personal* sense. I am not angry with him, or bitter, or resentful. However, I *have not* and *cannot* forgive him in the *legal* sense. He was tried and sentenced and is in prison serving the penalty imposed upon him for breaking the law. Only the State has the power to forgive him in the legal sense.

God's Word teaches that governments are here by God's permission and we should be subject to them. If we resist governmental authority, we are resisting an ordinance of God (Rom. 13:1-7).

Q: *Do you believe it was God's will for Diane to die in this horrible way?*

A: Many people blame God for the adverse circumstances which come into their lives and refuse to trust Him any longer. They believe He is unfair, unloving, and shows no compassion. For example, some people believe God is punishing them when excessive rains come, causing great damage.

But God is God, no matter what we may decide about Him. He does all things well. "Our God is in heaven; He does whatever pleases Him" (Ps. 115:3). We forget that we are in the ebb and flow of life, and we get the rain and thunder as well as the sunshine and warmth.

God is righteous and fair. "He causes His sun to rise on the evil and the good, and sends rain on the righteous and the unrighteous" (Matt. 5:45). Jesus said, "Do not worry about tomorrow, for tomorrow will worry about itself. Each day has enough trouble of its own" (6:34). God has honestly told us that each day may be filled with trouble. Why should we feel that we should be exempt from life's problems?

I believe God has a direct will for each life, yet He also allows tragedies and misfortunes to come which are not His direct will. He does not always intervene and keep accidents from happening. I am sure our daughter's assailant and God had not planned together to attack her. But even though He had the power to, God did not step between them to stop the murder. The sole responsibility for Diane's death rests on the one who caused it. God is in the clear.

When God is finished with us here, He takes us to heaven to be with Him. The way in which He accomplishes this is insignificant. I believe all of this was in God's overall plan for Diane, and we were part of that plan too. He had some very special and important instruction for us as well. And we continue to learn.

> "Father, forgive them," help me pray it,
> Tho they hate me without a cause,
> "Father, forgive them," help me say it,
> Tho they tear with fang and claws.
> "Father, forgive them," Jesus save them,
> For they "know not what they do."
> Help them learn from *my* forgiveness
> Of Thine *own* forgiveness too.

> J. SIDLOW BAXTER